T0289724

Crony Capitalism in US Health Care

The US political system has come to depend upon money too much. The US health care industry spends the most on political lobbying among all the 13 industrial sectors in the US economy. The government regulatory agencies at both federal and state levels have been 'captured' by the health industry interest groups meaning that the regulatory agencies respond to the interests of the industry but not those of the citizens.

This book employs a broad theoretical framework of crony capitalism to understand the US health care system dysfunction. This framework has not been applied before in any serious manner to understand the shortcomings in the US health care system. Specifically, the book examines the role of seven key players using this framework – politicians/interest groups, pharmaceutical companies, private health insurers, hospitals/hospital networks, physicians, medical device manufacturers, and the American public. Crony capitalism is a destructive force and is rampant in the US health care system, causing much waste, inefficiencies, and malaise in the system. Current efforts and initiatives, such as patient-centered medical homes and precision medicine, for improving/reforming the system, are of mere academic interest and tantamount to taking aspirin to treat cancer. They do not even pretend to address the root cause of the problem, namely, crony capitalism.

Offering prescriptions to fix the US health care system based on a comprehensive diagnosis of the dysfunction, this book will be of interest to researchers, academics, policymakers, and students in the fields of health care management, public and nonprofit management, health policy, administration, and economics, and political science.

Naresh Khatri is Associate Professor in the Department of Health Management and Informatics, School of Medicine, University of Missouri, Columbia, USA.

Routledge Focus on Business and Management

The fields of business and management have grown exponentially as areas of research and education. This growth presents challenges for readers trying to keep up with the latest important insights. *Routledge Focus on Business and Management* presents small books on big topics and how they intersect with the world of business research.

Individually, each title in the series provides coverage of a key academic topic, whilst collectively, the series forms a comprehensive collection across the business disciplines.

Crony Capitalism in US Health Care
Anatomy of a Dysfunctional System
Naresh Khatri

Entrepreneurship Education
Scholarly Progress and Future Challenges
Gustav Hägg and Agnieszka Kurczewska

Culture and Resilience at Work
A Study of Stress and Hardiness among Indian Corporate Professionals
Pallabi Mund

Optimal Spending on Cybersecurity Measures
Risk Management
Tara Kissoon

For more information about this series, please visit: www.routledge.com/Routledge-Focus-on-Business-and-Management/book-series/FBM

Crony Capitalism in US Health Care
Anatomy of a Dysfunctional System

Naresh Khatri

Routledge
Taylor & Francis Group

NEW YORK AND LONDON

First published 2022
by Routledge
605 Third Avenue, New York, NY 10158

and by Routledge
2 Park Square, Milton Park, Abingdon, Oxon OX14 4RN

Routledge is an imprint of the Taylor & Francis Group, an informa business

Library of Congress Cataloging-in-Publication Data
Names: Khatri, Naresh, author.
Title: Crony capitalism in US health care: anatomy of
a dysfunctional system / Naresh Khatri.
Description: New York, NY: Routledge, 2022. |
Series: Routledge focus on business and management |
Includes bibliographical references and index.
Identifiers: LCCN 2021011190 (print) | LCCN 2021011191 (ebook) |
ISBN 9780367631178 (hardback) | ISBN 9780367631185 (paperback) |
ISBN 9781003112204 (ebook)
Subjects: LCSH: Medical care, Cost of–United States. |
Medical economics–United States. | Medical policy–United States.
Classification: LCC RA410.53 .K54 2022 (print) |
LCC RA410.53 (ebook) | DDC 338.4736210973–dc23
LC record available at https://lccn.loc.gov/2021011190
LC ebook record available at https://lccn.loc.gov/2021011191

ISBN: 978-0-367-63117-8 (hbk)
ISBN: 978-0-367-63118-5 (pbk)
ISBN: 978-1-003-11220-4 (ebk)

DOI: 10.4324/9781003112204

Typeset in Times New Roman
by Newgen Publishing UK

To my sweet daughter, Avantika.

Contents

About the Author   ix
Preface   xi
Acknowledgment   xiv

PART 1
Explication of the US Health Care System Dysfunction   1

1   The Nature and Extent of the Problem   3

2   The Crux of the Problem   12

3   Medicine without Evidence   23

PART 2
Key Players Contributing to the US Health Care System
Dysfunction   29

4   Politicians/Interest Groups   31

5   Pharmaceutical Companies   38

6   Private Health Insurers   45

7   Hospitals and Hospital Networks   57

8   Physicians   69

  9 Medical Device Manufacturers   82

 10 American Public   86

PART 3
How to Fix the US Health Care System Dysfunction   93

 11 Addressing Crony Capitalism, Root Cause of the
     Dysfunction   95

 12 Health Insurance, Payment, and Pricing
     Arrangements   102

 13 Well-Informed Citizenry   112

     Conclusion   116

     Index   120

About the Author

Dr. Khatri earned his PhD in Organizational Behavior and Human Resource Management from the State University of New York, Buffalo, and MBA from the Indian Institute of Management, Ahmedabad. He is currently the professor of transformational leadership and strategic human resource management in the Department of Health Management and Informatics, School of Medicine, University of Missouri, Columbia. Before joining the University of Missouri, he was a faculty in the Nanyang Business School, Nanyang Technological University, Singapore. Dr. Khatri has authored/coauthored 4 scholarly books and published over 60 research articles and book chapters on health care management, strategic human resource management, leadership, strategic decision-making, and cross-cultural behavioral issues in reputed peer-reviewed journals. Three of his papers received nominations for the Best Paper Award at the Academy of Management. Several of his research articles have achieved the status of being classic because of their research impact. Dr. Khatri was the president of the Indian Academy of Management from 2018 to 2020. He has been on the editorial board of several peer-reviewed business management and health care management journals. He has received many research grants including a grant on HR and IT capabilities in health care organizations from the Agency for Healthcare Research and Quality (AHRQ) that was rated exceptional. In 2016, healthcareadministrator.org recognized Dr. Khatri as one of the top 50 health care administration professors in the US. Dr. Khatri is placed highly in the list that ranks faculty members according to the impact of their research in health policy and management programs in the US.

Preface

In this book, I employ a new, broad, and powerful theoretical framework of crony capitalism to understand the US health care system dysfunction. This framework has not been applied before in any serious manner to understand the shortcomings in the US health care system. Specifically, I examine the role of seven key players using this framework – politicians/interest groups, pharmaceutical companies, private health insurers, hospitals/hospital networks, physicians, medical device manufacturers, and the American public. I offer suggestions to fix the system based on a thorough diagnosis of the US health care system dysfunction.

I have had a long research and teaching career of over 30 years in studying all sorts of organizations and industries and a vast array of management theories. I have been researching and teaching health care organizations for the last 20 years. A deep understanding of the management literature combined with a thorough grasp of health care organizations provides me a unique perspective and insights into the US health care system and allows me to bridge these two broad fields. In this book, I draw from my long scholarly career involving research articles in top-tier journals and three scholarly books.

In 2001, I joined the Department of Health Management and Informatics, School of Medicine, University of Missouri, Columbia. My chief motivation in joining the Department of Health Management and Informatics was to apply my scholarly management expertise to improve the organization and management of health care organizations. To do so, I needed to understand the US health care system deeply. After my first five years or so of observing and researching health care organizations and the US health care system, I realized that there is a serious dysfunction in the US health care system and that this dysfunction was not an accident but driven by powerful forces.

It took me another five years or so when I began getting more clarity of the system's dysfunction. This happened as I researched on the topic of cronyism. I published influential research on cronyism in top-tier journals, namely, *Journal of Business Ethics* and *Journal of Internal Business Studies*. A natural extension of my research on cronyism was the key concept of crony capitalism. I found crony capitalism a powerful concept and my fascination with the concept culminated in a book in 2017 entitled *Crony capitalism in India: Establishing robust counteractive institutional frameworks.*

I grew up in India and my long stints in Singapore and US provided me a comparative perspective on economic, social, and cultural aspects of three different societies. Knowing both the Indian economic system and the US health care system, I noticed a striking similarity between the two. Both the systems are very big, complex, wasteful, and inefficient. Both have major governance problems. They suffer from ubiquitous greed, cronyism, and corruption. After coediting the book on crony capitalism in India, I felt that this framework applies equally well to the US health care system. Both the Indian economic system and the US health care system are a hodgepodge of capitalism and socialism. My understanding of both the systems suggests that the US health care system, like the Indian economic system, rather than combining the more desirable features of capitalism and socialism, which are efficiency and equality, respectively, has ended up combining the less desirable features of the two economic systems, which are greed and inefficiency, respectively.

My goal in this book has been to delve into the dysfunction in the US health care system and present it in a simple and clear manner that is easily accessible to a multitude of audience including scholars, policymakers and experts, teachers, and students of health policy, health economics, health administration, medicine, nursing, and political science. There seems to be a lot of ignorance and misinformation that prevent policy framers and citizens from making well-informed decisions about health care. In fact, the insiders of the system (pharmaceutical companies, hospitals, private health insurers, and physicians) would like to keep the status quo even if it is evident that the system is not serving the American society as well as it could. In this book, I seek to provide a clear and forthright understanding of the US health care system dysfunction and hope that such an understanding would lead to appropriate fixes to this mammoth problem, which is closing on $4 trillion annually and is about one-fifth of the US economy. Fixing the system offers potential savings worth a trillion of dollars or more annually.

This book has three parts. The first part of the book comprises three chapters that layout the problem comprehensively – the nature and extent of the problem, the crux of the problem, and medicine without evidence. The second part of the book consists of seven chapters each focusing on the role of one key player contributing to the system dysfunction – politicians/interest groups, pharmaceutical companies, private health insurers, hospitals and hospital networks, physicians, medical device makers, and the American public. The third part of the book offers suggestions to overcome the dysfunction and has three chapters – addressing crony capitalism, root cause of the dysfunction; health insurance, payment, and pricing arrangements; and well-informed citizenry.

Naresh Khatri
Professor of strategic human resource management and
transformational leadership
Department of Health Management and Informatics
School of Medicine
University of Missouri, Columbia

Acknowledgment

I am very grateful to the Department of Health Management and Informatics, School of Medicine, University of Missouri, Columbia, for supporting my scholarship over the last 20 years.

Part 1

Explication of the US Health Care System Dysfunction

The first part of the book attempts to explicate the US health care system dysfunction comprehensively and has three chapters – The Nature and Extent of the Problem, The Crux of the Problem, and Medicine without Evidence.

DOI: 10.4324/9781003112204-1

1 The Nature and Extent of the Problem

The last words of a coronavirus-infected patient before intubation, "Who's going to pay for it", capture fittingly the dismal state of the US health care system (Mahbubani, 2020). Americans are more worried about medical bills than even dying. In this chapter, I lay out the unsatisfactory state of the US health care system, which is a source of frustration and despair for so many Americans.

Overly Expensive, Unaffordable

Until the 1980s, despite spending much less on health care, Americans were doing better than other countries in their health outcomes (Frakt, 2018). Something happened to US health care spending after 1980. Confronted with fiscal pressures, as the share of gross domestic product (GDP) absorbed by health care spending began to get serious, other nations put measures in place to hold down spending but the US did not. The differential between what the US and other developed countries pay for prescriptions and for hospital and physician services has continued to widen over time. Suppliers of medical inputs marketed costly technological innovations (Callahan, 2009). They found ready customers in hospitals and medical practices eager to keep up with rivals in the medical arms race. In 1980, health care expenditures in the US were $256 billion, exploding to nearly $2.6 trillion in 2010, a tenfold increase (Meissner, 2013). Health care expenditures spiked further to $3.8 trillion in 2019. What began as a small gap in performance when compared to other countries is now a yawning chasm.

The per capita spending on health care in the US towers over all other developed nations, and yet health care outcomes as reflected by key health indicators are at best average. In other words, the US health care system consumes far more resources to produce the same or worse health care outcomes as compared to the health care systems elsewhere.

DOI: 10.4324/9781003112204-2

For example, the US spent $11,582 per capita in 2019 compared to $5,418 in Canada, $4,653 in the United Kingdom, $4,823 in Japan, and $4,224, the average of the Organization for Economic Cooperation and Development (OECD) countries (*OECD*, 2020). In total health care spending, the US spends 17.7 percent of its GDP, which is almost the double that of the average spending of 8.8 percent of GDP for the OECD countries.

In a comparison to the overall performance of the health care systems of 11 developed countries, the US was found dangling alone with high health care spending and low system performance (Schneider et al., 2017). Seven countries (Australia, Germany, the Netherlands, New Zealand, Norway, Switzerland, and the United Kingdom) bunch together and perform higher than the other four countries (Canada, France, Sweden, and the USA). Canada, France, and Sweden show mediocre performance with the US being the laggard.

The US health care system is a case of feast or famine. On the one hand, insured patients receive overly excessive care, generating mistakes and injuries that lead to about 30,000 deaths each year (Terhune, 2017). On the other hand, 45,000 deaths occur annually due to the lack of health care access; the lack of access has been suggested to be associated with a greater risk of death in uninsured adults by 40 percent (Meissner, 2013).

"The ballooning costs of health care act as a hungry tapeworm on the American economy" (Buffet quoted in *Associated Press*, 2018a). For example, over a decade (1999 to 2009), health care cost growth wiped out real income gains of nearly $5,400 per year for an average US family (Auerbach & Kellermann, 2011). If the US health care system could perform as that of the health care systems in other developed countries, an American would pay $4,000 to $6,000 less for health care costs per year.

The rising rates of health care insurance premiums prevent employees from getting any salary increases. For employer-sponsored health insurance, the costs keep creeping higher, leaving little or no money for employers to offer salary increases for their employees. From 1999 to 2009, while the average US salary grew by 38 percent, the health care premiums grew by a whopping 131 percent (*Healthcare Imperative*, 2010). The Centers for Disease Control and Prevention terms the increase in US health care costs over and above the general inflation in the economy as a 'greed factor'.

The system insiders – private health insurers, hospitals/hospital networks, pharmaceuticals/medical device makers, and physicians/ medical professionals – have successfully propagated the myth that the rising cost of health care in the US is due to an aging population

(Reinhardt, 2019), which is not quite true. The US, with one of the youngest populations among developed nations, has the highest per capita health care cost and more than double the per capita health care cost of Japan, which has one of the oldest populations in the world. The real driver of US health care costs is the per capita spending on health care (Horowitz, 2018).

According to a 2010 report by *Healthcare Imperative*, if prices of other commodities had grown as quickly as health care costs since 1945, a dozen eggs would cost $55, a gallon of milk $48, and a dozen oranges $134.

Back-of-the-envelope calculations comparing the prices of services and products in the US health care industry with other industries encapsulate how overpriced and inefficient the US health care system is. For example, if automobiles were priced similarly to services and products in the US health care industry, a midsize family car might cost about $200,000 or more. Similarly, if an airline industry priced its services like US health care providers, an airline ticket from New York to Los Angeles might cost something like $20,000 or $30,000 and the ticket might have to be purchased a year in advance and when you show up on the airport with your ticket, you might not find your seat or flight.

A Source of Anxiety, Insecurity, and Despair for Many Americans

The soaring costs of health care in the US are a source of severe financial burden and distress to Americans as evident from the fact that over 60 percent of all personal bankruptcies are medical (Himmelstein, Thorne, Warren, & Woolhandler, 2009). Most Americans, even those having insurance, are one major illness away from bankruptcy (Rosenthal, 2017).

A commonly unrecognized source of suffering for many Americans is health care insecurity. Health care insecurity is a sense of vulnerability, lack of control, and worry that individuals feel about getting the health care they need (Tomsik et al., 2014). As health care costs keep rising, more people seem to be skipping physician visits. Americans fear large medical bills more than they do a serious illness. Thirty-three percent of surveyed individuals in a study conducted by the University of Chicago and the West Health Institute were "extremely afraid" or "very afraid" of getting seriously ill (Gillies, 2018). About 40 percent said paying for health care was more frightening than the illness itself. Further, the survey found 54 percent of the participants received one or more medical bills over the past year for something they thought was covered by their insurance.

The fear of losing health care insurance undermines job and geographical mobility in Americans. For example, the Affordable Care Act, offering an option where individuals can get health insurance, has reduced 'job lock' or staying with a suboptimal job to keep health benefits, with an estimated 1.5 million people choosing to become self-employed as they can get an affordable health insurance of their own. A streamlined and integrated health insurance system that allows Americans to take their health insurance wherever they go could be quite liberating for them.

Wasteful, Starving Other Sectors of Economy

The US health care system on its current trajectory is *simply* unsustainable (*Institute of Medicine Report*, 2012; *OECD*, 2020). A recent review of 54 unique peer-reviewed research publications on the waste in the US health care system estimates the total annual waste to be in the range of $760 billion to $935 billion, accounting for approximately 25 percent of the total annual health care spending in the US (Shrank, Rogstad, & Parekh, 2019). This waste is more than the entire US defense budget in 2019. It is also more than the total Medicare spending in 2019. The estimated ranges of total annual cost of waste in the US health care system in the six commonly identified domains of waste are as follows: failure of care delivery ($102 billion to $166 billion), failure of care coordination ($27 billion to $78 billion), overtreatments ($76 billion to $101 billion), pricing failures ($231 billion to $241 billion), fraud and abuse ($56 billion to $84 billion), and administrative complexity ($266 billion).

The waste in the health care system, which is approaching a trillion-dollar mark annually, is wiping out efficiency, productivity, and wealth created by other industries and other parts of the US economy (Girod, Hart, & Weltz, 2018; Horowitz, 2018; *Manufacturing Institute*, 2013; *Milliman Medical Index*, 2020). A news article entitled "Health Care Will Bankrupt the Nation" sums up the extent of the problem in the US health care system rather well (Riedl, 2017). By straining national, state, and family budgets, the US health care system is contributing to the starvation of other vital sectors, such as infrastructure and education, which have contributed notably to America's wealth, ingenuity, and competitiveness:

"If the US budget collapses after hemorrhaging too much red ink, the main culprit will be rising health care costs", but not the entitlement programs such as social security (Horowitz, 2018). Absent some workable solution, spending on health care is likely to sink the federal budget, generating levels of debt that would hold back the economy and potentially spark a global crisis of confidence in United States' ability to borrow. Federal spending on health care (mostly Medicare and Medicaid) rose from 14.4% of all federal outlays in 1990 to about 31% in 2018 – one of the main reasons the national debt grew to $21.5 trillion in 2018 (Wolf-Mann, 2018). Alarmed by the costs of health care in the United States, the Chairman of the Federal Reserve, Jerome Powell, noted: "It's no secret: It's been true for a long time that with our uniquely expensive healthcare delivery system …, we've been on an unsustainable fiscal path for a long time" (quoted in Wolf-Mann, 2018).

One of the factors contributing to the decline of American manufacturing may very well be the high cost of health care in the US. In the ten years ending in 2012, employer costs for employee health care insurance increased by 66 percent – an increase in the structural cost disadvantage for US sfirms of 5.2 percentage points (*Manufacturing Institute*, 2013). Over the years, employer-provided health care costs have been growing much faster than the prices of products and services they sell. In 2018 in the US, the total cost of insurance for a typical family of four eclipsed $28,653, according to the *Milliman Medical Index* (2020). The employer contributed $16,368 and the employee contributed $12,285 ($7,703 as payroll deduction and $4,582 as out-of-pocket costs). The employer's contribution of $16,368 per employee adds to the cost of production in a significant way, making US manufacturing less competitive. One way to deal with the prohibitive costs of employee health care and to remain competitive for manufacturers is to move their production overseas.

A scrutiny of the 2018 uprising of school teachers across many states such as Arizona, Colorado, Kentucky, North Carolina, Oklahoma, and West Virginia suggests that the funding cuts due to rising health care costs over the last two decades underlie these resentments and uprisings (Yan, 2018). For example, protests in West Virginia were initially sparked by the state government taking away the health insurance coverage of school teachers. The cost of health care keeps rising at a much faster rate than the rate of inflation and increase in national income, thus leaving no money in state budgets for salary increases of teachers. School teachers across the nation have poor salaries and need to do other jobs, in addition to teaching, to be able to support themselves and their families. The annual waste in the US health care system of $760 billion to $935 billion is more than ten times the annual budget of the US Department of Education of $60 billion in 2019. Further, while the annual health care expenditure on Medicare in 2019 increased by 4.6 percent and projected to increase by about the same rate in 2020, the annual budget of the US Department of Education in 2019 shrank by $8 billion from 2018 and is expected to dwindle further in 2020.

Similarly, the US infrastructure – roads, airports, and power and electricity – has been deteriorating for quite some time. At one time, the US had by far one of the best infrastructures in the world, but not anymore. Even developing countries have either already caught up or catching up the US in the overall quality of their infrastructure. An international traveler is not likely to be too impressed with many airports in large US cities.

Unsafe, Poor Clinical Outcomes

Patient safety remains a major concern in the US. A study by researchers at the University of John Hopkins concluded that medical errors with 2,51,454 deaths annually was the third leading cause of deaths in the US after heart disease (6,11,105 deaths) and cancer (5,84,881 deaths), but well ahead of the fourth cause, chronic respiratory disease, with 1,49,205 deaths (Makary & Daniel, 2016). Why so many medical errors in US health care? They occur because of poorly coordinated care, fragmented insurance networks, and unwarranted variation in physician practice patterns that lack accountability.

The life expectancy in the US, a crude indicator of overall health of a nation, has shown a downward trend from 2015 to 2017: It fell in 2015, stayed level in 2016, and declined in 2017. Overall, the statistics show a downward trend in life expectancy in which Americans have lost 0.3 years of life. These statistics are a wakeup call that the US is losing too many of its citizens, too early and too often to conditions that are *preventable* (Sheridan, 2018). A baby born in 2017 in US is expected to live about 78 years and 7 months on average, which is three years shorter than a baby born in Canada.

The opioid crisis resulted in over 52,000 deaths in 2015, 64,000 in 2016, and 70,000 in 2017. A closer look suggests that most of these deaths were avoidable; they occurred because the US health care system was not functioning properly (*Associated Press*, 2018b). Similarly, the response to the COVID-19 pandemic suggests that the US health care system has performed rather poorly. The US having only 4 percent of the world population accounts for about 20 percent of the total number of COVID-19 global cases and deaths. A Sydney-based independent body, Lowry Institute, ranked the US a lowly 94 among 98 countries in COVID-19 response (Pandey, 2021).

Scam Like Features of US Health Care System

Chapter 2 considers that greed (crony capitalism or institutionalized corruption) may be the major driver of the US health care system dysfunction. The key players in the system have been successful in rigging the system to their advantage. The *Merriam-Webster* terms scam as a dishonest way to make money by deceiving people. The *Business Dictionary* defines a scam in a business setting as a fraudulent scheme performed by a dishonest individual, group, or company to obtain money or something else of value. The *Urban Online Dictionary* provides a more comprehensive definition of a scam: scam is a contrived scheme or process designed to surreptitiously, deceitfully, and materially benefit the perpetrators at the expense of the victims. A scam involves providing or selling goods or services, knowing them to be unfit for the purpose, while implying or claiming fitness in order to elevate the monetary value and generate undeserved revenue. A description of the US health care system by Belk (2018), a physician, sounds so similar to the definition of a scam:

> The simplest answer is that the money is going into the pockets of the many providers of health care. After all, for any great deception to work, all or most of the players in the deception have to be paid well enough to not ask too many questions or cause trouble. You can't run a major con game unless everyone necessary to make the con work is happy enough with their role to not want to cause trouble.

Conclusion

This chapter laid out the unhealthy state of the US health care system. The US health care system is causing pain and suffering and is a source of anxiety and insecurity in many Americans. It is inordinately expensive as a significant number of Americans find it beyond their means. For the last several decades, the rising costs of health care premiums have prevented employees from getting significant salary increases. Despite the US health care system being one of the most expensive in the world, it does not particularly render high quality and safe care as system insiders would like us to believe. It is wasteful and sucks vital resources from other critical sectors of the economy for its own maintenance. It has undermined the competitiveness of US manufacturers because high health care costs add to the cost of production and services. In sum, there is a serious dysfunction underlying the US health care system; it needs to be fully understood for it to be fixed, a topic explored in Chapter 2. It may not be an accident the way the system is. Powerful players seem to have contrived it the way it is and are deriving benefits in hundreds of billions of dollars every year.

References

Associated Press. 2018a. Amazon, Buffett, JPMorgan Chase tackle US health care tapeworm. January 30.

Associated Press. 2018b. CDC says life expectancy down as more Americans die younger due to suicide and drug overdose. November 29.

Auerbach, D.I. & Kellermann, A.L. 2011. A decade of health care cost growth has wiped out real income gains for an average US family. *Health Affairs*, 30(9): 1630–1636.

Belk, D. 2018. Conclusion: How did we get here and why is this so hard to fix? http://truecostofhealthcare.org/wp-content/uploads/2018/11/Conclusion.pdf

Callahan, D. 2009. *Taming the beloved beast: How medical technology costs are destroying our health care system.* Princeton University Press: Princeton, NJ.

Frakt, A. 2018. Medical mystery: Something happened to US health spending after 1980. *New York Times.* May 14.

Gillies, T. 2018. Why health care costs are making consumers more afraid of medical bills than an actual illness. *CNBC.* On the Money. April 22. www.cnbc.com/2018/04/22/why-health-care-costs-are-making-consumers-more-afraid-of-medical-bills-than-an-actual-illness.html.

Girod, C., Hart, S., & Weltz, S. 2018. *2018 Milliman Medical Index.* Milliman Research Report. Milliman: Seattle, WA.

Healthcare imperative: Lowering costs and improving outcomes. 2010. Workshop Series Summary (2010). Institute of Medicine of the National Academies: Washington, DC.

Himmelstein, D.U., Thorne, D., Warren, E., & Woolhandler, S. 2009. Medical bankruptcy in the United States, 2007: Results of a national study. *The American Journal of Medicine*, 122(8): 741–746.

Horowitz, E. 2018. The GOP plan to overhaul entitlements misses the real problem: To cut the debt – Congress needs to focus on health care costs. *FiveThirtyEight.com.*

Institute of Medicine Report. 2012. *Best care at lower cost: The path to continuously learning health care in America.* National Academic Press: Washington, DC.

Mahbubani, R. 2020. A New York anesthesiologist laments his coronavirus patient's last words before intubation: 'Who's is going to pay for it?' *Business Insider*. April 8.

Makary, M.A. & Daniel, M. 2016. Medical error—the third leading cause of death in the US. *The British Medical Journal*, 353: i2139.

Manufacturing Institute. 2013. *US health care costs are increasing*. www.themanufacturinginstitute.org.

Meissner, J. 2013. Unraveling the crisis in American healthcare. *Vital News* (Seattle), Spring.

Milliman Medical Index. 2020. *Milliman Research Report*. https://us.milliman.com/-/media/milliman/pdfs/articles/2020-milliman-medical-index.ashx.

OECD. 2020. *Health at a glance 2020: OECD indicators*. OECD Publishing: Paris.

Pandey, S. 2021. NZ, Taiwan top COVID performance ranking, US, UK languish. *Reuters*. January 27.

Reinhardt, U.E. 2019. *Priced out: The economic and ethical costs of American health care*. Princeton University Press: Princeton, NJ.

Riedl, B. 2017. Health care will bankrupt the nation. *U.S. News & World Report*. July 14.

Rosenthal, E. 2017. *An American sickness: How healthcare became a big business and how you can take it back*. Penguin Press: New York.

Schneider, E.C., Sarnak, D.O., Squires, D., Shah, A., & Doty, M.M. 2017. Mirror, mirror: How the U.S. health care system compares internationally at a time of radical change. *The Commonwealth Fund*. July.

Sheridan, K. 2018. US life expectancy drops again as overdoes climb. *AFP*. November 29.

Shrank, W.H., Rogstad, T.L., & Parekh, N. 2019. Waste in the US health care system: Estimated costs and potential savings. *JAMA*, 322(15): 1501–1509.

Terhune, C. 2017. Needless medical tests not only cost $200 billion, they can do harm. *CNN*. May 20.

Tomsik, P.E., Smith, S., Mason, M.J., Zyzanski, S.J., Stange, K.C., Werner, J.J., & Flocke, S.A. 2014. Understanding and measuring health care insecurity. *Journal of Health Care for the Poor and Underserved*, 25(4): 1821–1832.

Wolf-Mann, E. 2018. Powell: 'Our uniquely expensive healthcare' system will catch up with us. *Yahoo Finance*. September 26. https://finance.yahoo.com/news/powell-uniquely-expensive-healthcare-system-will-catch-us-212627406.html.

Yan, H. 2018. Here's what teachers accomplished with their protests this year. *CNN*. May 29.

2   The Crux of the Problem

Brill's (2013) observation offers a crucial insight into the US health care system dysfunction: When we debate health policy, we seem to jump right to the issue of who should pay the bills, blowing past what should be the first question: Why exactly are the bills so high? This chapter employs the broad theoretical framework of crony capitalism to answer the question raised by Brill and to explicate the underlying dysfunction in the US health care system. Three terms – greed, profit, and crony capitalism – could be used to describe the crux of the US health care dysfunction. These terms, however, are not the same.

Distinguishing Greed, Profit, and Crony Capitalism

Greed, a simple term that both a layman and an expert can easily comprehend, may explain a good deal of the dysfunction in the US health care system. Similarly, profit is another simple term that may capture much of the US health care system dysfunction in one word. The term profit as used here means profit made by rigging the system, which is different from the profit made in a fair, legal, and ethical manner.

Both greed and profit are much less precise terms and neutral to whether the dysfunction consists of random acts of corruption, or if the dysfunction is systemic and institutionalized. The dysfunction in the US health care system seems systematic and institutionalized. Thus, the term crony capitalism is preferred to either greed or profit.

As would become clear from the following discussions, greed in health care is widespread, being pursued brazenly by powerful system insiders, and is institutionalized. And to understand greed in the system, we need to grasp the dynamics of crony capitalism. Crony capitalism has resulted in a rigged US health care system and a tool of profit maximization for the system insiders at the expense of providing safe, affordable, and satisfactory quality of patient care to the US citizens.

DOI: 10.4324/9781003112204-3

Crony Capitalism

Crony capitalism is an extension of the generic concept of cronyism as it applies to businesses and firms in a nation or society (Khatri & Ojha, 2016). A politicized economic system is dubbed crony capitalist to distinguish it from a system of free markets and limited government. It is the deliberate, systematic use of public policy to manipulate markets in ways that benefit politically connected actors. Crony capitalism breeds rent seekers, stifles market entrepreneurs, and elevates unproductive activity to a higher cultural status than productive activity.

The entrepreneur's function is to reform or revolutionize the pattern of production. The entrepreneur does this by developing new goods and production methods, opening new markets, exploiting previously unused resources, and developing new ways of organizing business activities more efficiently (Mitchell, 2012). Unfortunately, in a crony capitalistic system, entrepreneurs innovate in socially unproductive ways. Unproductive entrepreneurship consists of finding new ways of rent seeking. For example, discovering a previously unused legal gambit that is effective in diverting rents to those who are first in exploiting it.

In crony capitalism, power and favors are wielded, exchanged, and acquired via an intricate system of personal contacts, favoritism, and championing of interests; the profitability of a business depends on political connections (Holcombe, 2012). Crony capitalism results when those in political power alter the structure of incentives that firms face by providing profit opportunities to individuals or firms who invest in political lobbying, campaigning, and relationships rather than in true profit opportunities (Olson, 1982). Cronies often stonewall the establishment of fair and transparent laws because such laws hamper their freedom to wheel and deal (Holcombe, 2012).

Crony capitalism engenders a higher return on developing lobbying and political skills – that is, becoming a crony – rather than on developing economically productive skills. Business activities in a crony capitalistic system end up in the hands of grifters or rent seekers or middlemen who are good at making political connections but not in the hands of market entrepreneurs who have new and better ideas, skills, and resources, and who are willing to take risks. Consequently, unimaginative, unproductive, inefficient, and wasteful economic initiatives, programs, and businesses are likely to spawn an economic system riddled with crony capitalism. Well-placed individuals (cronies) invest their vast fortunes in teams of lawyers, accountants, lobbyists, and political contributions to ensure that the system continues to work on their behalf (Salter, 2014). Lobbyists, political consultants, or grifters that advance the interests of crony firms command impressive salaries in such a system because their connections are worth it.

Crony capitalism has led US businesses, health care, education, criminal justice, and government to adopt practices that have bene-fitted a small segment of the population but harmed the majority (Johansson, Ryzina, & Embry, 2020). Salaries of executives of private health insurers, drug companies, and health care providers have been going through the roof while the patient care on all three dimensions of cost, access, and quality has suffered. There is a dramatic escalation in university administrators' salaries at the same time when the student debt is soaring. The practices of health care organizations and private educational institutions have taken advantage of patients and students (Johansson, Ryzina, & Embry, 2020).

Crony capitalism has several perverse effects (Gehl & Porter, 2020):

a **Erosion of overall business environment.** Political involvement of companies and interest groups is aimed at influencing economic pol-icies and regulations in ways that benefit particular industries, favor particular technologies, or advantage some companies and interest groups over others. Such efforts boost profits and advance special interests usually at the expense of larger public and economy.

b **Distortion of markets and undermining of open competition.** Corporate lobbying is damaging the healthy competition. The US historically pursued strict antitrust laws. Mergers and acquisitions in the same industry undermine competition. In recent years, the lax interpretation and enforcement of antitrust laws has resulted in an unprecedented number of industry mergers in the US. Both private health insurance and health care providers' markets have become super concentrated.

c **Erosion of social performance.** The disconnect between Wall Street and main street has been growing for a while. Now the gap is such that even a layman can see it. Because of the sole focus on profits and shareholders, there has not been much progress on crucial social policy priorities such as quality public education and afford-able health care. Corporations have undermined the performance of political system by enabling obstacles to healthy competition and undermining ethical and civic virtues (Gehl & Porter, 2020).

d **Normalization of unethical behavior.** A banker at Wall Street after receiving a fine and a sentence for an illegal act lamented that he felt too bad that he got caught. This banker was not ruing that he acted illegally, but what really bothered him was that he got caught. A major downside of capitalism is the preponderance of unethical behavior. Seeking self-interest with guile is the driving force. Without a guiding principle of ethics, capitalism can easily slip into crony capitalism and become greedy, vicious, and exploitative, what seems to have happened to the current US economic and health care systems. Business education and corporate culture glorify greed. Being nice, honest, ethical, and following the rules are for the weak. Day-to-day experiences in organizations of all kind seem to show contempt for whistleblowers and those stand against the wrong doings. Crony capitalism weakens the society by gnawing at civic virtues, ethical behavior, and character of its members.

Crony Capitalism Toolkit

In crony capitalism, the government actors influence the market for the benefit of their cronies and, by creating privilege, transfer wealth from the many to the favored few. Business-friendly legislation and regulatory rulemaking result from potentially perverse relationships between business and government. Although these relationships may be perfectly legal, they compose the crony capitalism toolkit: (a) campaign contributions to elected officials, (b) heavy lobbying of the Congress and rule-writing agencies, (c) a revolving door between government service and the private sector, (d) ballot initiatives at the state and local levels, and (e) involving employees in political activities (Gehl & Porter, 2020; Salter, 2014).

Gehl and Porter (2020) offer a couple of good examples of how companies use these tactics effectively to their advantage. From the late 1990s to 2017, citizen groups spent $4 million on lobbying for tighter restrictions on the sale of addictive painkillers. Drug companies, on the other hand, spent more than $740 million nationally to kill federal and state opioid regulations. Much of this funding was channeled through industry associations and third parties not subject to public reporting rules. The pharmaceutical industry succeeded in its efforts and its revenues soared, while more than 200,000 Americans died from opioid overdoses. In another example, in a ballot measure aimed at reducing prescription drug prices in California, citizen groups raised $10 million in support of the control, which is an impressive amount on the part of ordinary citizens, but drug companies spent more than $100 million opposing it. With such a lopsided matchup, the outcome of the ballot measure was a foregone conclusion.

These examples of throttling of efforts of well-meaning citizens for banning the sales of addictive drugs (opioids) and reducing prices of prescription drugs in California are quite instructive. Despite galvanizing and spending a lot of financial resources, ordinary citizen groups were no match for the drug companies with deep pockets. Such activities could be quite detrimental to a democracy. In fact, drug and health insurance companies wield such power and financial resources that they threaten political parties and candidates to toe the line or else.

The US Supreme Court's 2010 Citizens United decision is the chief culprit and has led to an explosion of corporate money into politics and a takeover of democracy by interest groups. American capitalism may have worked in the past because democratic forces acted as a check on greedy, exploitative instincts of capitalism. But democracy is likely to weaken in the face of unleashing of business and interest groups by the Supreme Court's Citizens United decision.

Crony Capitalism in the US Health Care System

Arguably, the US health care industry suffers from one of the highest levels of crony capitalism through a variety of well-established interest groups, and thus seems one of the best examples of this phenomenon. Large corporate insurers, health care providers, pharmaceutical giants, and physician associations wield intimidating influence through large political contributions (Harrington & Estes, 2008). Collectively, the medical industry is the largest lobbying force spending $604 million in 2019 alone, leaving other major lobbying industries such as oil and gas, security and investment firms, and defense and aerospace industry way behind (*Center for Responsive Politics*, 2020). It employed 2,826 lobbyists in 2019, which is the highest number among the 13 industrial sectors in the US economy (*Center for Responsive Politics*, 2020). There are many powerful interest groups in the industry that rank highly in their lobbying efforts.

Especially, five interest groups from the health care industry stand out and rank among the top 13 of the total 83 US industries in the amount of spending on lobbying in 2019: pharmaceutical firms (ranked #1 with 1,476 lobbyists), insurance (ranked #3 with 897 lobbyists), hospitals/nursing homes (ranked #9 with 807 lobbyists), physicians/health professionals (ranked #12 with 796 lobbyists), and health services/health maintenance organizations (HMOs) (ranked #13 with 815 lobbyists) (*Center for Responsive Politics*, 2020).

So many lobbyists prowling the health care landscape have turned the US health system into one big scam (see Chapter 1). In the case of the Affordable Care Act of 2009, insurance companies, pharmaceutical firms, hospitals and nursing homes, and physicians/medical professionals spent hundreds of millions of dollars lobbying the Congress to block key reform proposals that threatened corporate profits but would have made the act far more efficient and effective. Similarly, in the case of Affordable Care Act repeal in 2017, each senator comprising the small group of 13 senators responsible for formulating the repeal received an average of $214,000 campaign contribution from private health insurers and medical device manufacturers. The bills for the Affordable Care Act in 2009 and for its repeal in 2017 both were drafted in closed-door meetings by various interest groups, which tantamount to the fox guarding the henhouse. To term the US health care system as an orgy of interest groups may not be an overstatement.

The increasingly corporatized US health care system is driven by an insatiable appetite for profit (Brownlee & Saini, 2017). It is no longer about relieving the suffering of patients. It is about making money for pharmaceutical companies, device manufacturers, hospitals, insurance companies, and doctors. These players are gaming the system and hurting patients in the process. Doctors in the current corporatized health care system are pushed to be business people and give making money the same priority as upholding their oaths. The corporate imperatives to increase revenue result in worse patient care, higher costs, and less access.

Enormous Waste in the US Health Care System and What Underlies It

Three reputable studies have estimated the annual total waste in the US health care system. They suggest that the waste in the system ranges from 25 to 34 percent of the total health care expenditure annually. The Institute of Medicine report (*IOM Report*, 2010) estimated that about 31 percent of the total health care expenditure in a typical year amounts to waste. According to Berwick and Hackbarth (2012), the extent of waste in the US health system is about 34 percent of the total health care expenditure. Several other developed countries may have found a better solution to the health care problem than the US as they get same or better health care outcomes than the US by spending about half as much per capita and about half as much of their gross domestic product as the US (Schneider et al., 2017). Thus, the waste in the US health care system as high as 50 percent of the overall health care expenditure does not appear implausible. The latest study conducted by Shrank, Rogstad, and Parekh (2019) put a conservative estimate of the annual waste in the US health care system of about 25 percent of the total annual US health care spending. Even by this conservative estimate, with total health care expenditure in the US of $3.8 trillion in 2019, the amount of waste in the US health care system in 2019 works out to nearly a trillion dollars. This waste is more than the entire 2019 federal defense budget, and as much as the entire Medicare expenditure in 2019.

Four big drivers of the waste/dysfunction in the US health care system include administrative complexity ($266 billion), pricing failures ($235 billion), failures of care delivery and coordination ($130 billion to $244 billion), and overtreatments ($76 billion to $101 billion). Hospitals, pharmaceuticals, physicians, and private health insurers in various combinations contribute to most of the abovementioned waste in the system as discussed in the following paragraphs.

The first major driver of waste in the US health care system, administrative complexity, adds to an annual waste to the tune of $266 billion (Shrank, Rogstad, & Parekh, 2019). The biggest source of administrative complexity is private health insurance plans. The waste in the administrative complexity category consists of billing and coding to the tune of $248 billion annually. Because of the variety and complexity of private health insurance plans, health care providers need to employ an army of billing and coding clerks. While hospitals in other countries can do with half a dozen billing clerks and coding consultants, US hospitals require hundreds or even thousands of billing clerks. For example, Duke University's health system with 957 beds employs 1,600 billing and coding clerks (Reinhardt, 2019).

The second major driver of wasteful spending is pricing failures of health care procedures, drugs, and services. The waste because of pricing failures is estimated to be about $235 billion annually (Shrank, Rogstad, & Parekh, 2019). The US prices of most procedures, treatments, drugs, and services are at least twice or more than that of the identical procedures or services in other developed countries. This is so because of the absence of transparency and competitive markets in the US. Three major sources of price failures include highly overpriced drugs, overbilling or surprise billing, and more expensive treatments and procedures instead of equally effective cheaper treatments and procedures. The medication pricing failure contributes to the bulk of the waste to the tune of $170 billion. Drug companies are the ones that benefit most from the medication pricing failure, but health care providers also benefit to a significant extent. For example, a tablet of Tylenol at an academic medical center could be billed as much as $25. Health care providers also benefit from medication pricing failures by prescribing a new and more expensive drug for a treatment, where a cheaper and equally effective generic drug is available.

The third big driver of waste/dysfunction in the US health care system, the failures of care delivery and coordination, contributes to the annual waste in the system ranging from $130 billion to $244 billion (Shrank, Rogstad, & Parekh, 2019). This category of waste results chiefly from health care providers being poorly organized and managed and includes things like hospital-acquired conditions and adverse events, clinician-related inefficiencies, lack of adoption of preventive care practices, unnecessary admissions and avoidable complications, and readmissions. Chapter 7 suggested that the US health care providers lack a culture of innovation. Their business model is tilted toward making money by rigging the system through favorable health legislation rather than making money by being efficient and producing affordable, high-quality products and services. In the last couple of decades, health care providers have focused on mergers and acquisitions resulting in super concentrated hospital market in the US. Hospitals in such a concentrated market can operate inefficiently and provide poor quality of care and still thrive. It should come as no surprise that US hospitals are behind other industries in their management practices by at least a decade or more (Khatri, Pasupathy, & Hicks, 2012).

The fourth major driver of waste in the US health care system is the overtreatments with an estimated annual waste ranging from $76 billion to $101 billion. Overtreatments consist of unnecessary procedures, treatments, and services. The fee-for-service is chiefly responsible for the overuse as both physicians and hospitals can increase their revenue by prescribing more procedures and treatments (see Chapters 7 and 8).

Why is the US health care system not improving and the waste in the system keeps going up rather down? The plausible reason is that the national strategy to improve health care places too much emphasis on initiatives that are more of an academic interest and address at best peripherally what really ails the US health care system (Figueroa, Wadhera, & Jha, 2020). Most value-based programs have had no meaningful association with changes in cost, quality, or wasteful spending. For example, hospital pay-for-performance including the value-based purchasing and hospital-acquired condition reduction have not improved patient outcomes or reduced complications. Another program, the hospital readmissions reduction program shows little if any change in hospital visit rates, but modest unintended harm. Highly touted federal patient-centered medical home demonstrations have failed to generate any meaningful savings and improve the access, cost, and quality of patient care.

Two programs that currently are receiving much attention are translational science and precision medicine. These programs are not going to make any dent to the problem because either they also seem to be of mere academic interest or they do not speak to the core problem of crony capitalism in the US health care system. These programs would generate a lot of research activity and many scholars would get funded and advance their careers, but the system might not see the slightest improvement. Most of these programs are fads. We see a constant stream of fads in health care, a fad or two every year. Such programs amount to intellectual masturbation (Khatri et al., 2012). The *Urban Dictionary* defines intellectual masturbation as fascinating intellectual breakthroughs regarding reality, language, existence, knowledge, perception, or human behavior which are utterly without use, and therefore of no real consequence to anyone.

None of the big drivers of waste and inefficiencies is being addressed in any of the proposed health care reform initiatives. According to Berwick and Hackbarth (2012), of the possible explanations of the waste in the US health care system, the most plausible is politics or crony capitalism. While some call health care waste as 'waste', others call it 'income'. People and organizations (for-profit and not-for-profit) making money in the current system include powerful interest groups – hospitals, insurers, pharmaceuticals, and physicians – in a nation that tolerates strong influence in elections by big donors. When the big money in the status quo makes the rules, removing waste would translate into loss of income for the interest groups and loss of election for politicians. Naturally, both political parties hesitate to reform the system. For officeholders and office seekers in any party, it is simply not worth the political risk to try to dislodge even a substantial percentage of the US health care waste, even though the nation's schools, small businesses, road builders, scientists, individuals with low income, middle class people, would-be entrepreneurs, and communities could make much better use of that money (Berwick & Hackbarth, 2012).

Perhaps, the system is functioning the way the system insiders of the system have intended it. It has become a hodgepodge of capitalism and socialism, or socialism for the wealthy interest groups.

US Health Care System as a Peculiar Mix of Capitalism and Socialism

Ideally, when a system combines elements from two or more systems, it is supposed to borrow the desirable elements from each system. Unfortunately, the US health care system, rather than combining the best of capitalism and socialism, seems to have combined the worst of both. The strength of capitalism is efficiency, with greed being its downside. On the other hand, the strength of socialism is social equality and justice, with inefficiency and waste being its drawbacks. Put simply:

US Health Care System = Greed of Capitalism + Inefficiency of
Socialism

The government funding (funding by federal and state governments) now comprises almost half of the total health care spending in the US. Federal spending on health care (mostly Medicare and Medicaid) has risen from 14.4 percent of all federal outlays in 1990 to about 37 percent in 2019.

Conclusion

The US health care system is one of the best candidates for studying crony capitalism as it employs the largest number of lobbyists (2,826) and spends the most on lobbying ($604 million) annually among all the 13 US industrial sectors. The government regulatory agencies at both federal and state levels have been 'captured' by the health industry interest groups meaning that the regulatory agencies respond to the interests of the industry but not those of the citizens.

Crony capitalism in health care has resulted in massive waste/dysfunction in the system. A conservative estimate puts the amount of waste in the system as a quarter of total US health care expenditure of $3.8 trillion annually. But the waste could be as high as 50 percent of the total annual health care expenditure. This is because many other countries get the same or better health care outcomes than the US by spending about half as much per capita and about half as much of their gross domestic product as the US. The four big drivers of the waste/dysfunction in the US health care system include administrative complexity, pricing failures, failures of care delivery and coordination, and overtreatments. The four players that employ large number of lobbyists and spend a lot on lobbying annually chiefly contributing to the waste/dysfunction are private health insurers, hospitals, pharmaceuticals, and physicians. The US health care system, rather than combining the more desirable features of capitalism and socialism, has combined the less desirable features of the two economic systems. In a way, it has become socialism for the wealthy interest groups. Current efforts and initiatives to reform the system amount to giving aspirin to treat cancer. They are of mere academic interest and out of touch with respect to the root cause of the problem. They do not even pretend to address the root cause of the problem, crony capitalism, that is driving the waste, inefficiencies, and malaise in the US health care system. Many such efforts, in fact, unintendedly, appear to perpetuate rather than mitigate the US health care system dysfunction as they emanate from the same kind of thinking that has given rise to the current dysfunction.

References

Berwick, D.M. & Hackbarth, A.D. 2012. Eliminating waste in US health care. *JAMA*, 307(14): 1513–1516.

Brill, S. 2013. Bitter pill: How outrageous pricing and egregious profits are destroying health care. *Time*. March 4.

Brownlee, S. & Saini, V. 2017. Corrupt health care practices drive up costs and fail patients. *HuffPost*. May 26.

Center for Responsive Politics. 2020. Opensecrets.org.

Figueroa, J.F., Wadhera, R.K., & Jha, A.K. 2020. Eliminating wasteful health care spending – Is the United States simply spinning its wheels? *JAMA Cardiology*, 5(1): 9–10.

Gehl, K.M. & Porter, M.E. 2020. Fixing U.S. politics: What businesses can – and must – do to revitalize democracy. *Harvard Business Review*, July-August, 98(4): 115–125.

Harrington, C. & Estes, C.L. 2008. *Health policy: Crisis and reform in the US health care delivery system.* Fifth Edition. Jones and Bartlett Publishers: Sudbury, MA.

Holcombe, R.G. 2012. *Crony capitalism: By-product of big government.* Working Paper No. 12-32. Mercatus Center, George Mason University: Arlington, VA.

IOM Report. 2010. *The healthcare imperative: Lowering costs and improving outcomes.* Institute of Medicine of the National Academies: Washington, DC.

Johansson, B.M., Ryzina, M.V., & Embry, D. 2020. Scaling up and scaling out: Consilience and the evolution of more nurturing societies. *Clinical Psychology Review*, 81: 1–12.

Khatri, N. & Ojha, A.K. 2016. *Crony capitalism in India: Establishing robust counteractive institutional frameworks.* Palgrave Macmillan: Basingstoke, Hampshire, UK.

Khatri, N., Ojha, A.K., Budhwar, P., Srinivasan, V., & Varma, A. 2012. Management research in India: Current state and future directions. *IIMB Management Review*, 24: 104–115.

Mitchell, M. 2012. *The pathology of privilege: The economic consequences of government favoritism.* A working Paper. Mercus Center, George Mason University: Arlington, VA.

Olson, M. 1982. *The rise and decline of nations: Economic growth, stagflation, and social rigidities.* Yale University Press: New Haven, CT.

Reinhardt, U.E. 2019. *Priced out: The economic and ethical costs of American health care.* Princeton University Press: Princeton, NJ.

Salter, M.S. 2014. *Crony capitalism, American style: What are we talking about here?* Working Paper 15-025. Edmund J. Safra Center for Ethics, Harvard University: Boston, MA.

Schneider, E.C., Sarnak, D.O., Squires, D., Shah, A., & Doty, M.M. 2017. Mirror, mirror: How the U.S. health care system compares internationally at a time of radical change. *The Commonwealth Fund.* July.

Shrank, W.H., Rogstad, T.L. & Parekh, N. 2019. Waste in the US health care system: Estimated costs and potential savings. *JAMA*, 322(15): 1501–1509.

3 Medicine without Evidence

When patients go to see a doctor, they take it for granted that the doctor has the latest knowledge of medicine and that the procedure or treatment that they are being prescribed is evidence-based and the most appropriate of all that are currently available in cost and quality. However, a typical, everyday encounter between a patient and a physician is far from the ideal notion of a physician and medical practice. What most patients may not realize is that the treatment or procedure that they are receiving may not be based on evidence, or be the most appropriate in its efficacy and cost. This issue is an important one from the perspective of a high-performing health care system and thus needs attention.

Evidence-based Medicine

Evidence-based medicine means the conscientious, explicit, and judicious use of current best evidence in making decisions about the care of individual patients (Patashnik, Gerber, & Dowling, 2017). According to the National Academy of Medicine, evidence is the cornerstone of a high-performing health care system. Modern medicine seems to have pulled off a remarkable coup in that it has convinced an unsuspecting public that the interventions delivered by its physicians are uniformly based on scientific evidence (Leifer, 2014). But the fact is that *less than half* of all medical care in the US is based on adequate evidence about its effectiveness (Gibson & Singh, 2010; Leifer, 2014; Newbergh, 2006; Patashnik, Gerber, & Dowling, 2017; Prasad et al., 2013; Rosenthal, 2017), suggesting that the lack of incorporation of evidence-based medicine in their everyday practice by physicians remains a problem in the US (Patashnik, Gerber, & Dowling, 2017; Rosenthal, 2017). Many treatments and procedures are adopted or discarded based on physicians' personal experiences or what treatment or procedure is in fashion at the time rather than based on science or evidence (Newbergh, 2006).

DOI: 10.4324/9781003112204-4

It is not uncommon to find examples of treatments or procedures that had no clear scientific rationale meaning they were not effective in curing the ailment, but became popular and frequently prescribed (Prasad et al., 2013). The use of arthroscopic surgery to treat osteoarthritis of the knee became a preferred method of treatment in the mid-1980s. However, a robust randomized placebo-controlled trial concluded that a surgical procedure performed on millions of patients to ease the pain of arthritic knees worked no better than a fake operation.

In 1989, without any clear scientific rationale, some doctors began experimentally treating metastatic breast cancer patients using the bone marrow transplant procedures (Leifer, 2014). About 15 to 20 percent of the patients died from the drugs used in the procedure. Many others had permanent injuries, including heart damage and hearing loss. On top of that, the procedure cost upward of $200,000. Despite the lack of evidence supporting the procedure's efficacy, as well as it being highly expensive and having potentially catastrophic side effects, the procedure saw an explosive growth over the next two decades.

The bispectral index (BIS) monitor became commonly used without sufficient medical evidence (Prasad et al., 2013). Although rare, anesthesia awareness (or intraoperative awareness) is debilitating and is associated with post-traumatic stress disorder and anxiety. The BIS monitor was developed to measure the level of consciousness accurately to ensure that patients receive adequate anesthesia. The Food and Drug Administration (FDA) approved the device in 1997 and by 2007 half of all operating rooms in the US were using it. However, in 2008, a large, randomized trial comparing the BIS monitor with a standardized sedation monitoring strategy found no benefit for the device.

Stenting for stable coronary artery disease was a multibillion-dollar-a-year industry before it was found to be no better than the medical management for most patients with stable coronary artery disease. Similarly, the hormone therapy for postmenopausal women intended to improve cardiovascular outcomes was found to be worse than no intervention. The list of such popular inefficacious treatments is long. A large study examining 363 treatments found that only 138 of them (38 percent) were effective, whereas 146 (40 percent) were ineffective (Prasad et al., 2013).

Comparative Effectiveness Research

The comparative effectiveness research considers comparing two or more health care interventions – such as a drug, a diagnostic test, or a surgical procedure – to determine which intervention works best for which patients (Patashnik, Gerber, & Dowling, 2017). Health care markets fail to function efficiently if physicians and patients lack reliable information about the comparative effectiveness of treatment options. Yet, a significant fraction of the medicine that Americans consume still uses minimal scientific evidence about its comparative effectiveness. Many treatments offer only minor benefits over alternatives but come with an exorbitant price tag.

The relative lack of emphasis on comparative effectiveness research seems more by tacit design by the players involved in the health care system than by accident. For example, the Patient-Centered Outcomes Research Institute is not allowed to establish what type of health care is cost-effective (Patshnik, Gerber, & Dowling, 2017).

A relatively new player in the market is the pharmacy benefit management. The pharmacy benefit management companies are for-profit that make money by negotiating discounts with drug manufacturers. The items that end up on the formularies of covered drugs and devices of pharmacy benefit managements are not always the ones patients need most or those that work best, but rather the ones on which the pharmacy benefit management has wrangled the best deal, with the best negotiated profit margin (Rosenthal, 2017).

In the last 20 years, fewer new molecular entities have been launched on the market every year, with the majority of new drugs offering little or no therapeutic advance over existing products (Gagnon, 2013).

Starting in 1992, the Prescription Drug User Fee Acts made the FDA dependent on funding from pharmaceutical firms, deepening its regulatory capture (see Chapter 5). The pharmaceutical industry demands more rapid reviews of applications to market new drugs that result in an epidemic of insufficiently tested drugs, many of which prove to be harmful and even to have fatal side effects that are undiscovered until they are in general use (Rodwin, 2013).

The FDA's drug approval process is problematic from the perspective of comparative effectiveness because the agency's mission does not include weighing one drug against another but, rather, merely approving a new drug if it works at all, even if it has no advantage over cheaper drugs already on the market (Deyo & Patrick, 2005). The FDA's process for approving medical devices is even more lax as agency notes as part of its policy: "New devices are less likely than drugs to have their safety established clinically before they are marketed".

Why Evidence-based Medicine and Comparative Effectiveness Research Receives So Little Attention?

The same dynamic of crony capitalism that underlies the overall US health care system dysfunction undermines evidence-based medicine and comparative effectiveness research. In terms of players, drug companies, hospitals, insurers, and medical device manufacturers all contribute to the problem.

A nation not evaluating the comparative effectiveness of treatment alternatives to help reduce waste and improve quality, and such evidence not affecting clinical and policy decisions point toward major defects in the overall institutional apparatus of the nation (Patashnik, Gerber, & Dowling, 2017). Political incentives (lobbying, campaign contributions) and the misuse of professional authority by physicians have undermined the efforts to tackle the medical evidence problem and curb wasteful spending.

Medicare and private health insurers should ideally stop paying for a medical treatment that unbiased experts agree provides no benefit and may cause harm. Unfortunately, the health care industry and many in the medical profession prefer not to apply scientific evidence for the public benefit because they would lose income (Gibson & Singh, 2010). These days treatments follow not scientific guidelines, but the logic of commerce in an imperfect and poorly regulated market, whose big players spend more on lobbying than defense contractors (Rosenthal, 2017).

The glut of treatments of early adoption of controversial and unproven forms of treatment is suggestive of greed in the health care system (Leifer, 2014). Developing new drugs is a time-consuming and costly enterprise and it is not financially rewarding. The pharmaceutical industry's business model thus does not rest as much on therapeutic innovations as on manipulating the systems through patents and coming out with drugs that have minor variations of existing drugs that could be sold at high prices as new drugs (Gagnon, 2013). Further, much research evidence has accumulated indicating that, because of the conflict of interest, physicians are prone to prescribe unnecessary, less effective, more expensive treatments to their patients (see Chapter 5).

Entrenched Culture of Consuming More Health Care

Anything, even the slightest bruise, the go-see-your-doctor syndrome and the culture of frequent health checkups have all created much more demand for health services, many of which are unnecessary and expensive. If doctors are ethical and basic services are cheap, such a health care model can work effectively. To see the doctor for unnecessary aspects of health has created a culture where healthy people who have no health issues and do not need a checkup feel guilty that they have not seen a doctor.

While Americans may believe more care is better, research suggests that more medicine may be worse (Gawande, 2009). This is because nothing in medicine is without risk. Complication can arise from hospital stays, medications, procedures, and tests, and when these things are of marginal value, the harm can be greater than the benefits (Gawande, 2009). But again, the overuse of medical services and procedures is a good business for those who provide them. This kind of culture and made-up dependence on the system contributes to the waste in the system.

Guidelines for checkups and medical procedures are geared at least partly to generate a constant stream of income for the physicians of particular specialties. For example, the way car dealers approach state legislatures requiring yearly car inspections. The car safety inspections may not improve the safety of cars on the roads, but they do contribute to more income for car dealers.

'Evidence-based' guidelines are published by various medical specialties. The purpose of many of these documents is to protect the specialties' financial stake in the system. For example, the 'unholy alliance' among big pharmaceutical firms, the FDA, and the diagnostic and treatment guidelines published by the American Psychiatric Association has been suggested to distort the science underlying psychiatric diagnostic and treatment, thus resulting in significant social injury (overdiagnosis and overtreatment) (Cosgrove & Wheeler, 2013).

Conclusion

The two basic essentials of a high-performing health care system are the following: medicine be practiced based on scientific evidence and the prescribed treatments and procedures be more effective and less costly than alternative procedures and treatments. Yet *less than half* of all medical care in the US is based on adequate evidence about its effectiveness. There continues to be widespread utilization of tests and treatments that are unproven and possibly useless, or even harmful to the patients. Further, the treatments and procedures that patients are prescribed are not necessarily more effective, but are surely more expensive than other available treatments and procedures.

References

Cosgrove, L. & Wheeler, E.E. 2013. Drug firms: The codification of diagnostic categories, and bias in clinical guidelines. *Journal of Law, Medicine & Ethics*, Fall, 644–653.

Deyo, R.A. & Patrick, D.A. 2005. *Hope or hype: The obsession with medical advances and the high cost of false promises.* AMACOM Books: New York.

Gagnon, M.A. 2013. Corruption of pharmaceutical markets: Addressing the misalignment of financial incentives and public health. *Journal of Law, Medicine & Ethics*, Fall, 571–580.

Gawande, A. 2009. The cost conundrum. *The New Yorker*. June 1.

Gibson, R. & Singh, J.P. 2010. *The treatment trap: How the overuse of medical care is wrecking your health and what you can do to prevent it.* Ivan R. Dee: Chicago.

Leifer, J. 2014. *The myth of modern medicine: The alarming truth about American health Care.* Rowman & Littlefield: Lanham, MA.

Newbergh, C. 2006. The Dartmouth atlas of health care. In S.L. Isaacs & J.R. Nickman (eds.), *Robert Wood Johnson Foundation Anthology: To improve health and health care*, pp. 25–48. Jossey-Bass: San Francisco.

Patashnik, E.M., Gerber, A.S., & Dowling, C.M. 2017. *Unhealthy politics: The battle over evidence-based medicine.* Princeton University Press: Princeton and Oxford.

Prasad, V., Vandross, A., Toomey, C. et al. 2013. A decade of reversal: An analysis of 146 contradicted medical practices. *Mayo Clinic Proceedings*, 88(8): 790–798.

Rodwin, M.A. 2013. Introduction: Institutional corruption and the pharmaceutical policy. *Journal of Law, Medicine & Ethics*, Fall, 544–552.

Rosenthal, E. 2017. *An American sickness: How healthcare became a big business and how you can take it back*, Penguin Press: New York.

Part 2

Key Players Contributing to the US Health Care System Dysfunction

This part of the book consists of seven chapters with each chapter focusing on one of the seven key players that contribute to the US health care system dysfunction – politicians/interest groups, pharmaceutical companies, private health insurers, hospitals and hospital networks, physicians, medical device manufacturers, and the American public.

DOI: 10.4324/9781003112204-5

4 Politicians/Interest Groups

The US political system has come to depend on money too much. Political parties and candidates need to raise tons of money to be competitive and win elections. The reality they face is that they have got to begin raising money for the next term the day after they have been elected for the current term. The packing order, chairing or being a member of an influential congressional committee, depends upon who brings in more political donations. Such a political environment is a perfect playground for grifters.

Since Supreme Court's Citizens United decision in 2010, the money in politics has been pouring at a mind-boggling scale. It seems that no amount of money is enough to contest an election. Nearly $24 billion were spent by federal candidates, political action committees (PACs), and party committees in the 2020 US election (Enten, 2021). In 2016, the amount spent was $9 billion. Presidential candidates alone raised $4 billion in 2020 compared to $2 billion in 2008. The North Carolina senate race in 2020 saw a spending of $265 million by the two candidates and outside groups. The Iowa senate race involved a total spending of $218 million. The House races are no pushovers. In 2018, $42 million was spent in California's 39th District race and, in 2020, about $37 million was spent in New Mexico's 2nd District.

Why business groups donate this pile of money to US elections? Politicians from both major political parties are heavily dependent upon the money that they receive from the business and interest groups. In exchange, these business and interest groups want their pound of flesh. Chapter 2 makes the case that crony capitalism (or the government-granted favors) is a destructive force. It misdirects resources, impedes genuine economic progress, and breeds corruption. Business and interest groups do not seek the same policies as average citizens do, rather their positions on issues are aligned against the citizens. For example, citizens want drugs at lower, more affordable prices but drug

DOI: 10.4324/9781003112204-6

companies want to keep prices high and they do not want the federal government to negotiate drug prices on behalf of citizens. The groups that donate a lot of money to political campaigns are found to be less attentive to consumer needs. Their products, services, and ideas are not good enough to compete in the free market (Mitchell, 2012). Thus, to ply their business, these business and interest groups spend efforts and resources to rig policy and rules in their favor. The failure of American political institutions, because of the undue influence of interest groups, lies at the heart of the US health care system dysfunction (Harrington & Estes, 2008).

Lobbying profession in the US has become increasingly more lucrative pointing toward increasing graft in the economy. The extent of how well the lobbying profession is doing in the US may be evident from the fact that five of the richest counties in the US are in the suburbs of the District of Columbia where majority of the lobbyists reside. I once happened to visit the state capitol in Jefferson City, the capital of Missouri. The most striking feature of my visit was the sheer number of well-paid lobbyists that I encountered in the hallways. There are over a thousand lobbyists registered at Jefferson City, a town with a population of about 43,000. Any company worth its salt, whether small or large, operating locally or nationally or internationally, has one or more lobbyists lobbying for them. Ordinary citizens need to be worried whenever legislators are in session since the legislative session is the time for politicians and interest groups to conduct their business.

Spending on Lobbying and Number of Lobbyists in the Health Care Industry

The US health care system is a customary playground for politicians and interest groups as the health care industry employed the largest number of lobbyists (2,826) and spent the most amount on lobbying ($604 million) among all the 13 US industrial sectors in 2019 (*Center for Responsive Politics,* 2020). Pharmaceuticals/health products, health insurance companies, hospitals/nursing homes, physicians/health professionals, and health services/ health maintenance organizations (HMOs) ranked #1, #3, #9, #12, and #13, respectively, among 83 US industries in the amount of money spent on lobbying in 2019 (*Center for Responsive Politics,* 2020). Politicians have become heavily dependent upon the health care industry for their political careers and the industry has become a piggy bank for political parties and candidates. The White House and members of Congress open the public coffers wider and deeper every year to favor the lobbyists who help them get reelected.

Campaign contributions are one of the best bargains in Washington. The return on an investment of thousands of dollars in campaign contributions is millions or billions of the dollars of the public money (Gibson & Singh, 2010). There is a growing realization that crony capitalism has become rampant, and powerful business and interest groups have captured the American democracy and political institutions (Mitchell, 2012; Salter, 2014).

The Capture of US Health Policy by Business and Interest Groups

The University of Chicago economist George Stigler won the Nobel Prize in economics for showing that regulatory agencies are routinely 'captured' and used by the firms they are supposed to be regulating.

Patashnik, Gerber, and Dowling (2017), in their book, *Unhealthy Politics: The battle over evidence-based medicine*, lament that the US health care system continues to produce inefficient outcomes year in, year out without triggering an effective response. It is characterized by bad science, inconsistency, and waste. *Less than half* of all medical care in the US is based on adequate evidence about its effectiveness. There continues to be a widespread utilization of tests and treatments that are unproven and possibly useless, or even harmful to the patients (see Chapter 3). The authors lay the blame for the continued poor performance and status quo in the US health care system squarely upon the failure of the American political system, because of too much polarization, bickering, and pettiness, and upon the misuse of authority by the medical profession.

The health care industry is exempt from the rigor of the US free-market system (Weissman, 2016). When you ask the price of any health care service, you will receive the same answer: 'What insurance do you have?' Billing is not determined by how much a treatment or procedure costs but rather how much can be extracted from each patient on a case-by-case basis. It is a rigged, predatory system that is built on undermining free markets through political influence. Outsize profits, salaries, and bonuses that many players in the health care industry enjoy are not driven by their contributions to great health care but by the concentration of market power, political entanglement, and private intermediation of public policies (Lin & Neely, 2020).

Because the increasingly corporatized health care system is driven by an insatiable appetite for profit, the US health care system is no longer about relieving the suffering of patients or the intrinsic value of maintaining the health of the population (Brownlee & Saini, 2017).

It is about making money: for pharmaceutical companies, device manufacturers, hospitals and other health care providers, health insurance companies, and doctors. These players have gamed the system via lobbying for favorable policies and legislations at both federal and state levels that is hurtful to larger public. Even more serious is the fact that crony capitalism has come to be accepted as normal in a system that professes to care about nothing but the welfare of patients.

Rosenthal (2017), in her book entitled *An American sickness: How healthcare became a big business and how you can take it back*, notes that, in the past quarter century, the American medical system has stopped focusing on health or science but instead has attended single-mindedly to its own profits. The patient care, healing, and safety do not seem to be the primary considerations, but rather a by-product. Faced with disease, Americans are potential victims of *medical extortion* (Rosenthal, 2017). The US health care is not a system but an industry and at every point there is a way to make more money. A recent example of an egregious behavior that headlined news is the case in which a father was billed for $32 for holding his son upon delivery.

While it began with the American Medical Association, there are now so many narrow, specialized medical groups, each spending prolifically to promote their particular interests. Specialty medical societies are flush with money and have formed their own super PACs. Despite being relatively new, some of them now give as much or more money than the AMPAC, the super PAC of the American Medical Association. Some notable super PACs of medical societies include radiologists (RADPAC), Neurologists (BrainPAC), orthopedics (Orthopedic PAC), cardiologists (ACC PAC), family medicine (FamMedPAC), dermatology (SkinPAC), and emergency medicine (NEMPAC).

Gilens and Page (2014) examined various theories of American politics on the influence of elites, interest groups, and average citizens and concluded that corporations and business and professional associations dominate the US interest group universe and these interest groups as a whole do not seek the same policies as average citizens do. In fact, their stands tend to be negatively related to the preferences of average citizens. Further, these business and professional interest groups spend much more money and tend to get their way as far as the US policy formulation and implementation are concerned. The authors suggest that their study findings constitute troubling news for advocates of 'populistic' democracy, who want governments to respond primarily or exclusively to the policy preferences of their citizens. For example, 90 percent of Americans support a legislation that allows the federal government to negotiate drug prices. But politicians from both national parties do not bring such a legislation for consideration because of the campaign contributions that they receive from drug companies (Jorgensen, 2013; Whitaker, 2018). Additionally, politicians fear that doing so would anger drug companies who can mount a vicious advertising campaign against them during their elections (Whitehouse & Sinnett, 2017).

According to Whitehouse and Sinnett (2017), the US government has been infiltrated and disabled by corporate interest groups and dark money. Business groups, such as pharmaceutical firms, have done so using some of the following means: (a) striking fear in elected representatives who do not 'get right' by threatening million-dollar dark money election attacks; (b) stacking judiciary in business-friendly ways; (c) capturing the administrative agencies meant to regulate corporate behavior; and (d) creating a corporate alternate reality on public health and safety issues via spreading misinformation.

Institutional Sclerosis

Olson (1982) proposed the thesis of sclerosis. Sclerosis is excessive resistance to change. Institutions that fail to adapt and change at a sufficient pace are sometimes described as displaying institutional sclerosis. Institutional sclerosis seems to aptly explain the current state of the US health care system and many of its interest groups. Olson claims that 'pure' capitalism, if it even exists, becomes politically 'sclerotic' by the slow accretion of protection arrangements organized by narrow, specific interest groups. The accumulation of vested interests and rent seekers ultimately slows the ability of a government to reform, adapt, and secure perfectly competitive markets. This sclerosis saps an industry's and economy's dynamism.

Conclusion

Money has become the oxygen of American political system. Corporations, businesses, and trade and professional associations dominate the US interest group universe and these interest groups do not seek the same policies as average citizens do. Interest and preferences of citizens tend to diverge from those of the business and interest groups. That is why, despite an overwhelming support of citizens for many important societal issues, they do not get legislated by the Congress. In this sense, the US health care system is a customary playground for politicians and interest groups. Many powerful interest groups in the industry have rigged the system by capturing health policy. The US health care industry employs the largest number of lobbyists and spend the most amount on lobbying among all the 13 US industrial sectors. Pharmaceutical companies, private health insurers, hospitals/ nursing homes, health professionals, and health services/HMOs are the five groups in the health care industry that spend the most on lobbying. The US health care system continues to perform poorly because of its capture by powerful interest groups and the highly polarized and dysfunctional American political system that remains at the mercy of large political donations from wealthy, powerful business and interest groups.

References

Brownlee, S. & Saini, V. 2017. Corrupt health care practices drive up costs and fail patients. *HuffPost*. May 26.

Center for Responsive Politics. 2020. Opensecrets.org.

Enten, H. 2021. How Trump made people care about politics again. *CNN*. January 2.

Gibson, R. & Singh, J.P. 2010. *The treatment trap: How the overuse of medical care is wrecking your health and what you can do to prevent it*. Ivan R. Dee: Chicago.

Gilens, M. & Page, B.I. 2014. Testing theories of American politics: Elites, interest groups, and average citizens. *Perspectives on Politics*, 12(3): 564–581.

Harrington, C. & Estes, C.L. 2008. *Health policy: Crisis and reform in the U.S. health care delivery system*. Fifth Edition. Jones and Bartlett Publishers: Sudbury, MA.

Jorgensen, P.D. 2013. Pharmaceuticals, political money, and public policy: A theoretical and empirical agenda. *Journal of Law, Medicine & Ethics*, Fall, 561–570.

Lin, K.H. & Neely, M.T. 2020. *Divested: Inequality in the age of finance*. Oxford University Press: New York.

Mitchell, M. 2012. *The pathology of privilege: The economic consequences of government favoritism*. A working Paper. Mercus Center, George Mason University: Arlington, VA.

Olson, M. 1982. *The rise and decline of nations: Economic growth, stagflation, and social rigidities*. Yale University Press: New Haven, CT.

Patashnik, E.M., Gerber, A.S., & Dowling, C.M. 2017. *Unhealthy politics: The battle over evidence-based medicine*. Princeton University Press: Princeton and Oxford.

Rosenthal, E. 2017. *An American sickness: How healthcare became a big business and how you can take it back*. Penguin Press: New York.

Salter, M.S. 2014. *Crony capitalism, American style: What are we talking about here?* Working Paper 15-025. Edmund J. Safra Center for Ethics, Harvard University: Boston, MA.

Weissman, S.I. 2016. Perspective: Skyrocketing health care costs are caused by political corruption. *Center for Health Journalism.* June 21.

Whitaker, B. 2018. EX-DEA agent: Opioid crisis fueled by drug industry and congress. *CBS News, 60 Minutes.* June 17.

Whitehouse, S. & Stinnett, M.W. 2017. *Captured: Corporate infiltration of American democracy.* New Press: New York.

5 Pharmaceutical Companies

For much of the medical history and into the 1980s, drugs were cheap and the people running pharmaceutical companies were interested in social impact as well as money. But the character of the drug discovery changed in the mid-1990s when the Food and Drug Administration (FDA) and the US Patent and Trademark Office established a patent system with no pricing restrictions on drugs. The flawed patent system, in the name of rewarding innovation, has offered undue protection and monopoly to manufacturers in pricing their drugs. A consequence has been that many bestselling medicines today are covered by more than five patents, and some by more than a dozen. Seventy-four percent of cancer drugs approved by the FDA during the previous decade ultimately did not extend life by even a single day (Rosenthal, 2017) and there are persistent shortages of cheaper, affordable, essential medicines in hospitals. Pharmaceutical firms have come to personify crony capitalism. They have rigged the health care system to their advantage in alliance with other key players, especially politicians and physicians.

The Nexus between Drug Companies and Politicians

As back as 1995, Thompson noted that pharmaceuticals have few peers when it comes to the use of money in influencing rules. In the intervening years, they have become more emboldened, refined, and brazen in their endeavors. Thompson calls the underlying dynamics as dependence corruption: the Congress members depend upon campaign contributions to get elected. Campaign contributions in turn come in large part from industries and wealthy individuals who stand to profit from laws and regulations that stem from Washington.

Pharmaceutical companies have perfected the art of crony capitalism (Richtman, 2018). They employed 1,476 lobbyists and spent $299 million

DOI: 10.4324/9781003112204-7

in lobbying in 2019 alone, ranking #1 in both categories among 83 US industries (*Center for Responsive Politics*, 2020). Two of their major lobbying groups are Pharmaceutical Research and Manufacturers of America and the Biotechnology Innovation Organization. The pharmaceutical firms – the manufacturers, wholesalers, distributors, and chain drugstores – now have an influence over Congress that has never been seen before (Whitaker, 2018). During the 2018 midterm elections, pharmaceutical companies along with physicians and medical professionals gave $225 million to federal candidates, outside money groups, and political parties (*Center for Responsive Politics*, 2018).

Jorgensen (2013) explains how pharmaceutical industry has captured the legislative process and owns the legislators at both state and federal levels. Pharmaceutical manufacturers donate money directly to candidates, political parties, and political action committees, and they also fund outside spending organizations or spend money separately on the candidate or political party such as for buying TV ads. Most of the campaign contributions go to incumbents, to those in the majority party, and to those who sit in the congressional committees important to the industry – a pattern entirely consistent with the intention of seeking legislative favors. A result of the control of pharmaceutical companies over legislators is that, despite there being well-researched and documented solutions to the commonly noted problems in the drug development process – such as the development of me-too drugs, unethical conduct in clinical trials, selective disclosure of clinical-trial data, and payments to doctors for prescribing certain drugs – they do not get legislated (Jorgensen, 2013).

The Nexus between Drug Companies and Physicians

The culture of medical profession and its public health mission are being undermined by the pharmaceutical industry's wide-ranging influence (Cosgrove & Wheeler, 2013). Over the last two decades, the dominant business model of major pharmaceutical companies has been characterized by massive spending on promotion, especially an explosion of promotion of pharmaceuticals directed toward physicians. The US pharmaceutical industry spends up to $42 billion in promotion toward physicians every year to influence their prescribing habits and generate profits (Gagnon, 2013). Thus, physicians' prescribing habits may be informed not only by clinical evidence but also by marketing and corruption of science (Shah & Fugh-Berman, 2013). In many ways, one can say that the evidence-based medicine has been replaced by the marketing-based medicine.

An extensive literature describes how pharmaceutical firms use financial and nonfinancial inducements to influence physicians' attitudes and decisions (Shah & Fugh-Berman, 2013). Financial inducements include honoraria, gifts, speakers' fees, unrestricted educational grants, and sponsored research. Nonfinancial inducements include the use of deference, the opportunity to be revered as an expert, and publication productivity facilitated by industry-funded ghostwriters.

The Compromised FDA

Starting in 1992, the Prescription Drug User Fee Act made the FDA dependent on funding from pharmaceutical firms, deepening its regulatory capture (Rodwin, 2013). The industry demands more rapid reviews of applications to market new drugs resulting in an epidemic of insufficiently tested drugs, many of which have harmful side effects (Rodwin, 2013). The interactions between the FDA and industry concerning specific medical products have included a minimal number of experts and been conducted away from the public view (Califf, 2017).

The system at the FDA is unique in the degree to which industry sets the terms of agenda, pointing to its regulatory capture (Carpenter, 2017). The FDA is first and foremost a public agency. However, the operations of the FDA suggest as if it is a body owned by drug companies. The FDA appears to treat the drug industry as a customer that it needs to please, instead of acting as a regulator to ensure the public health (Hilzenrath, 2016). The FDA places too much emphasis on getting drugs approved quickly and not enough on making sure they actually work and work safely. In 2015, the FDA approved 95 percent of all new medicines submitted for review on the first try, which was up from 36 percent in 1993.

The industry continually lobbies the FDA to increasingly look beyond data from controlled clinical trials when assessing drugs. The industry is using sophisticated sounding buzzwords 'patient-reported outcomes', 'real-world evidence', and 'novel clinical trial designs' to dilute the robust standards for determining the efficacy of new proposed drugs. Such approaches are far from scientifically sound and more susceptible to manipulation and lowering the standards of approval (Hilzenrath, 2016).

At other federal agencies that rely heavily on user fees, paying a fee buys companies the right to conduct business – but not to negotiate with their regulator. For example, at the Securities and Exchange Commission, user fees are a cut-and-dried affair. If a firm wants to sell stocks or bonds, it must pay the Securities and Exchange Commission a registration fee, much like a tax. Similarly, the Nuclear Regulatory Commission uses a hands-off approach. It recoups about 90 percent of its annual appropriation through various fees, some of which are levied on operators of nuclear power plants (Hilzenrath, 2016). When the Nuclear Regulatory Commission proposes the fee amounts each year as part of a standard rulemaking process, the companies responsible for paying the fees can submit public comments – just like everyone else.

The Pharmaceutical Benefit Manager

A new player in the US health care system, pharmaceutical benefit manager (PBM), has emerged. A PBM is a third-party administrator of prescription drug programs. In theory, PBMs, as giant buying networks for drugs, are supposed to reduce health care costs because of their bargaining power to negotiate lower prices of drugs with manufacturers and pass part of the savings to consumers. But the reality is more complicated. PBMs get billions of dollars each year in rebates from pharmaceutical companies to help them "select" which brand name medications to put on their formularies (Belk, 2018). So, instead of selecting the most cost-effective medications, PBMs are encouraged to select medications that yield higher rebates, which usually means selecting more expensive medications.

Lack of Innovation

A common refrain is that drugs are more expensive in the US because of the costs associated with developing new drugs. Unfortunately, there is an innovation crisis in the pharmaceutical research and development (Gagnon, 2013; Thompson, 1995). In the last 20 years, a minority of 'new' drugs represent a therapeutic advance over products already available; much of the research budget goes toward minor variations on existing pharmaceuticals rather than looking for biological breakthroughs (Gagnon, 2013). The profit motive in the pharmaceutical sector does not seem to encourage the development of new drugs as the main way to increase earning capacity as innovation is a risky, time-consuming business (Alpert, 2005; Gagnon, 2013).

Corrupting of Science

It is not only the public but even the medical profession has also been duped through the manipulation of research to support questionable drugs. Leifer in his book, *The myth of modern medicine*, noted:

There's a growing body of evidence to suggest the gross manipulation of research is used to support the approval and subsequent
sales of drugs. The manipulation includes both the outright falsifi-
cation of data and the suppression of key research findings – leading
to the misinterpretation of a drug's efficacy or safety. Rather than
being rare events, some of these practices appear to be standard
operating procedures within the industry.

(2014; p.167)

The Opioid Crisis

Pearl (2017), a physician and ex CEO of the Permanente Medical
Group, in his book, *Mistreated: Why we think we're getting good health
care and why we're usually wrong*, delineates the contours of the US
opioid crisis. He notes that this opioid crisis did not happen by chance
but is the result of a deliberate effort by drug manufacturers to shift
doctors' perception in favor of prescribing more of these dangerous
medications. Pharmaceutical manufacturers were engaged in aggressive
marketing of opioids that helped promote their overuse. In one notable example, more than 5,000 clinicians attended 40 all-expenses-paid
pain conferences in which Purdue Pharma promoted extended-release
oxycodone (OxyContin). Due to these and other marketing activities,
annual sales of extended-release oxycodone grew to exceed $2 billion
(Vikinger, 2018). As the sales of the opioids soared, so did the number
of Americans dying of opioid overuse. The opioid crisis resulted in over
52,000 deaths in 2015, 64,000 in 2016, and 70,000 in 2017.

Doctors were assured by manufacturers that these drugs are safe and
do not cause addiction. This led to users of these drugs to take them
for life. Doctors were also offered lucrative financial incentives for prescribing these drugs. The assertions about the protection from addiction
and resistance to overdose proved to be wrong, but thousands of patients
lost their lives because of the overdose and dependence on these drugs.

The drug problem in the US cannot be resolved until the policies
address the real wrongdoers of the drug crisis: Big Pharma (Ghanem
2018). To solve the problem requires actions against drug-making and
selling giants such as Purdue Pharma, McKesson, Insys Therapeutics,
Cardinal Health, and AmerisourceBergen. Morrissey, Mayor of
Rockford, Illinois, in his interview on *CBS News* in 60 Minutes with
Lesley Stahl noted:

The drug companies don't advertise, hey we're raping you. We're
taking advantage of you. We're exploiting children and abusing

taxpayers. They don't talk that way, right? Although that's what the net effect is of what they're doing ... They are bunch of crooks.

(Stahl, 2018)

Generic Drug Manufacturers Have Come to Play the Game Too

The whole idea behind the generic drugs is that they, being much cheaper than the brand name (prescription drugs), would bring down the costs of drugs. Unfortunately, the executives of companies making generic drugs have learnt from their counterpart brand name drug manufacturers how the US health care system works. The generic drug manufacturers settle into a price range that is slightly lower than that of the brand names, which is not all that helpful given the exorbitant prices of brand name drugs (Rosenthal, 2017).

Conclusion

Pharmaceutical firms are the personification of crony capitalism and the resulting greed and dysfunction in the US health care system. Thanks largely to their money influence, the pharmaceutical industry is one of the most profitable businesses in America. Pharmaceutical companies employ the greatest number of lobbyists and spend the most on lobbying, ranking them #1 in both categories among 83 US industries. Pharmaceutical firms rig the health care system in alliance with other key players in the system, especially politicians and physicians. A myth is propagated that if drugs are expensive in the US, it is because of the costs associated with research and innovation. The arguments offered in this chapter suggest that the contrary is true. There is rather a lack of new drugs. Drug companies are labeling existing drugs with minor variations as new drugs. This allows them charging higher prices. Drug companies have also contributed to the corruption of research and science. The FDA is too subservient to pharmaceutical firms. It, thus, ends up serving the interests of drug companies rather than the larger American public.

References

Alpert, B. 2005. Roche's revolution. *Barron's*, 85(14): 20–22.
Belk, D. 2018. *Conclusion: How did we get here and why is this so hard to fix?* http://truecostofhealthcare.org/wp-content/uploads/2018/11/Conclusion.pdf

Califf, R.M. 2017. Transparency at the U.S. Food and Drug Administration. *Journal of Law, Medicine & Ethics*, 45(S2): 24–28.

Carpenter, D. 2017. FDA transparency in an inescapably political world. *Journal of Law, Medicine & Ethics*, 45(S2): 29–32.

Center for Responsive Politics. 2018. Opensecrets.org.

Center for Responsive Politics. 2020. Opensecrets.org.

Cosgrove, L. & Wheeler, E.E. 2013. Drug firms: The codification of diagnostic categories, and bias in clinical guidelines. *Journal of Law, Medicine & Ethics*, Fall, 644–653.

Gagnon, M.A. 2013. Corruption of pharmaceutical markets: Addressing the misalignment of financial incentives and public health. *Journal of Law, Medicine & Ethics*, Fall, 571–580.

Ghanem, D. 2018. Guest Commentary: If you want to take on drug dealers, start with big pharma. *The Missourian.* April 6.

Hilzenrath, D.S. 2016. FDA depends on industry funding: Money comes with "string attached". December 1. www.pogo.org/investigation/2016/12/fda-depends-on-industry-funding-money-comes-with-strings-attached/

Jorgensen, P.D. 2013. Pharmaceuticals, political money, and public policy: A theoretical and empirical agenda. *Journal of Law, Medicine & Ethics*, Fall, 561–570.

Leifer, J. 2014. *The myth of modern medicine: The alarming truth about American health Care.* Rowman & Littlefield: Lanham, MD.

Pearl, R. 2017. *Mistreated: Why we think we're getting good health care-and why we're usually wrong.* Public Affairs: New York.

Richtman, M. 2018. Big pharma's cash flood is drowning seniors. *CNN.* April 3.

Rodwin, M.A. 2013. Introduction: Institutional corruption and the pharmaceutical policy. *Journal of Law, Medicine & Ethics*, Fall, 544–552.

Rosenthal, E. 2017. *An American sickness: How healthcare became a big business and how you can take it back.* Penguin Press: New York.

Shah, S. & Fugh-Berman, A. 2013. Physicians under the influence: Social psychology and industry marketing strategies. *Journal of Law, Medicine & Ethics*, Fall, 665–672.

Stahl, L. 2018. The problem with prescription drug prices. *CBS News, 60 Minutes.* May 6.

Thompson, D.F. 1995. *Ethics in Congress: From individual to institutional corruption.* The Brookings Institution: Washington, DC.

Vikinger, K.N. Opioid crisis in the US – Lessons from Western Europe. 2018. *Journal of Law, Medicine & Ethics*, 46: 189–190.

Whitaker, B. 2018. EX-DEA agent: Opioid crisis fueled by drug industry and congress. *CBS News, 60 Minutes.* June 17.

6 Private Health Insurers

The private health insurers along with pharmaceuticals/medical device makers, hospitals/hospital networks, and physicians/medical professionals form the core of the US health care system. Thus, both the credit and the blame for the way it is lie with them.

Most countries allow, and some encourage, the private insurance as an upgrade to second tier to a higher class of service and to a fuller array of services. However, the private health insurance companies are heavily regulated requiring them to offer uniform fees to customers to prevent them from engaging in more pernicious forms of practices (Quadagno, 2008). This is not the case in the US, where the private insurance companies are allowed to use sophisticated forms of medical 'underwriting' to set premiums and skim off more desirable employee groups and individuals. The American system of financing health care has far strayed from the basic concept of insurance, which was to spread risk over a large pool of policy holders so that everyone, regardless of age or wealth, paid the same amount for coverage (Potter, 2010).

US is the only nation that fails to guarantee coverage of medical services, rations extensively by ability to pay, and allows the private insurance industry to serve as a gatekeeper to the health care system. In general, health insurance used to be about giving people access to health care. Now it is about giving providers access to patients (Gibson & Singh, 2010). It is hard to think of a more unfair financial arrangement between the patients and the health care system, one in which the buyer side is virtually defenseless vis-à-vis the supply side, and it is hard to imagine that any other country would allow it (Reinhardt, 2019).

The chief concern of private health insurers in the US has been to prevent the federal government from creating competing products and programs. This chapter discusses the length to which the private health insurers go, the tactics that they employ to keep their hegemony, and thwart any meaningful reform of the US health care system.

DOI: 10.4324/9781003112204-8

A History of Undermining Health Care Reform

The health insurance companies have been at the core of the resistance to any meaningful reform of the US health care system. They have run misinformation campaigns and taken advantage of the goodness of Americans. There have been many attempts by popular leaders to reform the system. Every time the insurance companies have scared American voters by ramping up the slogan of 'socialized medicine' or the US becoming a 'communist nation'. Unfortunately, it has worked almost every time as discussed briefly in the following section. The 'socialism' or 'communism' or 'government takeover of medicine' or 'US health care system is the best in the world' rhetoric is escalated any time there is any discussion of reforming the US health care system.

The Internal Revenue Service gave an impetus to the employer-sponsored health insurance in the US in 1943 by ruling that it should be tax free. With that ruling, the health insurance benefits became an expectation of all employees because it was less expensive for employers to purchase health insurance for employees than for employees to buy it themselves (Chapin, 2017).

By the end of World War II, the health insurance companies had grown large enough to have powerful lobbies. Harry Truman discovered this the hard way in 1945 when he proposed a nationalized health insurance program similar to the one being implemented in the UK. The private health insurance companies joined hands with the American Medical Association in a campaign to defeat Truman's plan in Congress (Belk, 2018). They attacked the bill by running a national campaign accusing Truman of trying to make US a communist nation by turning health care into a government-controlled system. The campaign worked so well that the bill was defeated and Democrats suffered a sound defeat in the 1946 mid-term elections.

In 1962, John Kennedy attempted to broaden the health insurance coverage to cover those who could not get private coverage. To avoid any confrontation with the private health insurers, Kennedy proposed to provide insurance to those people to whom private insurance companies did not want to cover: the elderly, the disabled, and the poor. The private health insurers, however, perceived any competition by the government as a direct threat to their business and decided to nip it in the bud. So, they again partnered with the American Medical Association to defeat Kennedy's bill. The campaign warned Americans that the 'Medicare' bill would be the first step toward socialism and would eventually rob Americans of their freedom. The campaign worked again and Medicare was killed only to be revived by Lyndon Johnson in 1965.

Johnson had a supermajority of Democrats, 68 Democrats in Senate and 295 Democrats in the House (Belk, 2018). So, he managed to get the Medicare bill through Congress. This is the only time the insurance companies and the American Medical Association suffered a defeat.

Jimmy Carter tried to expand the Medicare in 1980 but failed. Richard Nixon and Bill Clinton wanted to provide universal health care to American citizens by making private insurance more afford-able and available, but they too failed to get any legislation passed. After defeating Clinton's health care reform, insurers felt that the coast was clear for them to abandon nonprofit practices, long-standing commitments to public service, and traditional insurance models and turn instead to satisfying Wall Street investors' desire to make money (Potter, 2010).

Barack Obama did pass the Affordable Care Act because it did not offer any government option at the insistence of private health insurers. While the legislation covered individuals with preexisting conditions, it did not have any provisions to control the greed of the players that have largely contributed to the dysfunction. Basically, the Affordable Care Act ended up covering more people with the same unsustainable costs and wastes, thus making the US health care system to consume even more resources.

Chapin (2017) argues that the American Medical Association invented "the company insurance model" as an alternative to govern-ment intervention. According to her, the association made a bargain with the devil, and the US health care system has been forever suffering from the greed of the private insurance companies.

As physicians' antipathy to national health insurance dwindled – tempered by the benefits of guaranteed payment, split among various specialty groups, and loss of allies among other health professionals and employer groups – health insurers have moved to the forefront of the resistance to reform the health care system (Quadagno, 2008). Now the private insurers control the US health care system, making health insurance as the most expensive in the world. Insurance companies have gradually moved beyond financing medical services to also managing medicine.

The Medicare does well in controlling the administrative costs in a significant manner; however, it too suffers from the problems inherent in the system, such as the physicians continue to be paid for every ser-vice they provide, thereby encouraging them to over-deliver care to the insured. The prices of services, procedures, and products for reimburse-ment that the Medicare uses are the ones set by the private, for-profit association, namely, the American Medical Association.

The Linchpin of the US Health Care System Cabal

The US spending on health care reached $3.8 trillion in 2019, or about $11,582 per person. The private health insurance with an expenditure of $1.2 trillion accounted for 31 percent of this spending. Hospitals too accounted for 31 percent of the health care spending with an expenditure of $1.2 trillion. Physician and clinical services are the third largest spenders accounting for 20 percent of the spending with $772 billion. These three players spend a lot on lobbying and they also benefit from tacit nexus among them (Gibson & Singh, 2010; Ryun, 2018).

Intuitively, insurers should be shutting down the gaming of the system, if they want to save money. But big hospitals hold enormous leverage in setting terms of insurance contracts, because insurers need them in their networks. For example, the largest private health insurer, United Health Group, by coopting with hospitals and physicians has built a huge network of one million physicians and 6,000 hospitals. By creating win–win arrangements with physicians and hospitals, the United Health Group has built a big empire with a lot of monopoly power (Brownlee & Saini, 2017; Ryun, 2018). In the process, it has done little to curb the shockingly high prices of health care procedures and services. Insurance companies control much of the money that goes into health care. That means that the more the health care costs, the more power they have (Belk, 2018).

Insurance companies are the linchpin of the cabal that has developed in the US health care system. They know that the more expensive and unaffordable it becomes, the more it creates a need out of fear to be insured just in case a major illness strikes and bankrupts individuals and their families. Insurers have realized that the best way to make money in health care is to bottleneck care that ought to be inexpensive while making it appear as though they are judiciously stewarding scarce resources. They have rigged the system in a way that allows them to win every time they make things worse for everyone (Belk, 2018). While the role of other players and how they contribute to the US health care system dysfunction is relatively easy to grasp, it is not all that easy to decipher how the private health insurers contribute to the dysfunction. They have kept things opaque and complex, and strategically coopted other players by spreading money around (Belk, 2018). Potter (2010) lays out the hideous deception of the private health insurers in his book, *Deadly spin*.

Deadly Spin

Potter offers insights into how private health insurers have rigged the US health care system to their advantage. Here, I borrow some of the key points from his book to reveal the underhand dealings that the private health insurers resort to. Potter, in his long career as an executive in the public relations offices of Humana and CIGNA, two major private health insurers, portrays a compelling picture of the extent of dishonesty and corporate propaganda that private health insurers propagate to influence how the public thinks and how the lawmakers vote. Over the last several decades, the industry has used various tactics effectively to create a perception of its critical role and usefulness in providing health care and obscuring its real goal of profits and greed.

Broadly, the industry employs two-pronged public relations strategy to achieve its objectives. One prong entails a highly visible 'charm offensive' designed to create the perception of the industry as an advocate of health care reform and a good-faith partner in improving the US health care system. The second prong of the strategy consists of secret, fearmongering campaign using business and political allies to aggressively disseminate misinformation and lies, with the sole intent of killing any reform that might hurt industry's profits.

The key elements of the American health insurance companies' playbook include the following: (a) distract people from the real problem or question whether there really is a problem by making false assertions such as the US health care system is the best in the world; (b) generate fear by making unfounded claims such as the government-run health systems around the world are falling apart and forcing patients to forego treatments; (c) encourage people to doubt truth, facts, and scientific conclusions; and (d) say one thing in the public while working secretly to do the opposite such as raising intentionally insurance premiums that go to pay high salaries to their executives but professing to be the 'victims' of the rising health care costs because of aging and the use of modern technologies (Potter, 2010).

The private health insurers devote resources and employ numerous time-tested tools and strategies to maintain the status quo. One effective tactics that they have borrowed from the big tobacco and military–industrial complex is the 'third party technique', which involves creating subversive grassroots or front groups that discredit legitimate individuals or organizations, spread false information, distort truth, and instill fear. Potter (2010) provides an example of one such group, namely, the Center for Consumer Freedom which claims that its mission is to defend the rights of consumers to eat, drink, and smoke as they please. In reality, this center is a front group for tobacco, restaurant, and alcoholic beverage industries and promotes their agenda.

The private health insurers form political coalitions with like-minded organizations – small business owners, pharmacists, or insurance agents – to create 'grassroots' social movement activities and fund public campaigns designed to convince politicians that the public opposes reform (Quadagno, 2008).

During the heat of the affordable health care reform of 2009, the insurance industry ran well-organized grassroots groups to get people out to disrupt the town halls of Congressmen. The member companies of America's Health Insurance Plans recruited an estimated four hundred thousand seniors, who participated in town hall meetings, contacted members of Congress through phone calls, emails, and letters, and were flown to Washington to lobby for the insurers (Potter, 2010). In one of the town halls, one woman said she had heard that some people working behind the scenes on the legislation had close ties to communists. Another woman said she had heard all the pizzeria owners in the area would be put out of business if health reform legislation passed. Grassroots groups avoid listing funding sources and use misleading, feel-good names that stress patriotism, individual freedom, or American values.

Big American health insurers employ large public relations department and use independent public relations agencies as well. The best public relations are those that are invisible and use insidious techniques to manipulate public opinion and public policy (Potter, 2010). The health insurance industry pays consultants and pollsters millions of dollars to craft and test phrases in focus groups and surveys that could be used in spreading misinformation. For example, the industry has found that the phrases 'the best health care system in the world' and 'a government takeover of the health care system' resonate with public. Thus, the industry uses them often in their misinformation campaigns to sway public opinion.

Public relation departments of health insurance companies cultivate mutually beneficial relationships with TV and newspaper reporters. They control access to major newsmakers in business and government and use it as a leverage in promoting stories/misinformation that advance the interests of the industry. They sponsor fearmongering and misleading ads, coordinate attacks by conservative opinion columnists and health policy experts for hire, and pay groups that run anti-reform ads and orchestrate political events. They prepare nice briefing packets for rehash by lawmakers, the industry's allies, talk show hosts, and editorial writers. Potter (2010) calls these public relations efforts as a spin machine and notes that the public relations executives of health insurance companies make the KGB look amateurish.

And of course, the private health insurance companies shower members of the Congress with political contributions and overwhelm them with hundreds of lobbyists to push their agenda. In 2019 alone, these insurance companies employed 897 lobbyists and spent $156 million in political contributions, ranking third in both categories out of the 83 industries in US (*Center for Responsive Politics*, 2020). At the time of affordable care legislation, from 2007 to 2009, private health insurance companies spent $586 million and at the height of the battle, the industry spent about $7,00,000 daily (Potter, 2010).

The private insurers work hard to cultivate an image of kind and caring folks who think only of you and your health and are working hard as real partners with the Congress and the White House to find "a uniquely American solution" to what ails the system (Potter, 2009). In truth, the private health insurers resort to devious, dishonest, and unethical public relations practices that further their self-interest at the expense of the American people and the democratic principles this country was founded on.

Potter's (2009) caution is worth noting:

> Remember this: whenever you hear a politician or pundit use the term "government-run health care" and warn that the creation of a public health insurance option that would compete with private insurers (or heaven forbid, a single-payer system like the one Canada has) will "lead us down the path to socialism", know that the original source of the sound bite most likely is some public relations department of a private health insurer.

The major media and academia are heavily influenced by the hegemonic ideology of corporate America and they play along with the private health insurers. Not only the *New York Times* (whose editorial board includes several CEOs of insurance companies) but also the *Washington Post* and the major television networks marginalize and ridicule the single-payer position, presenting it as "extreme", "utopian", and the like (Navarro, 2008). Affluent Americans are a big part of the problem by supporting tag lines of private health insurers (see Chapter 10).

Administrative Complexity

In their study on the waste in the US health care system, Shrank, Rogstad, and Parekh (2019) estimated that the total annual waste in the health care system ranged from $760 billion to $935 billion. The administrative complexity, among the six domains of waste, contributed the most to the annual waste to the extent of $266 billion. In terms of waste due to administrative complexity, the billing and coding contributed

$248 billion annually, which could be attributed mostly to the variety and complexity of private health insurance plans. The price of a particular procedure varies widely among the insurers for a given hospital, and among hospitals, for a given insurer. Moreover, even for one hospital, the price of a given procedure paid by a given insurer varies by the type of insurance policy the patient has.

Just what drives these huge price variations? There is no empirical evidence showing any correlation between these prices and the quality of health care delivered, nor is there any correlation with the production costs. The reason is that the health care marketplace has been distorted by insurance companies wielding concentrated power because of their unique role as both sellers of insurance and buyers of health care services. Insurers run roughshod over weaker health care providers and independent doctors. The individualized contracts with health care providers and insurance plans are designed to extract every penny possible from both the patients and health care providers. Doing so makes the health care system administratively complex. Aaron, a distinguished health economist, describes the system rather well:

> I look at the U.S. health care system and see an administrative monstrosity, a truly bizarre mélange of thousands of payers with payment systems that differ for no socially beneficial reason, as well as staggeringly complex public systems with mind-boggling administered prices and other rules expressing distinctions that can only be regarded as weird.
>
> (quoted in Reinhardt, 2019)

Because of the variety and complexity of private health insurance plans, the health care providers need to employ an army of billing and coding clerks. While hospitals in other countries can do with half a dozen billing clerks and coding consultants, the US hospitals require hundreds or even thousands of billing clerks. For example, Duke University's health system with 957 beds employ 1,600 billing and coding clerks (Reinhardt, 2019).

Administrative costs of private health insurance plans in the US are 15 percent as compared to 5 percent for the Medicare and Medicaid. The dramatically higher administrative costs in the US than in Canada reflect the inefficiencies (such as complex and costly billing systems) of the US private insurance-based, multi-payer system. Physician practices in Ontario, Canada, spent $22,205 per physician per year interacting with Canada's single-payer agency – just 27 percent of the $82,975 per physician per year spent in the US (Reinhardt, 2019). The US nursing staff spent 20.6 hours per physician per week interacting with health plans – nearly ten times that of their Ontario counterparts. According to Himmelstein, Campell, and Woolhandler's study (2020), if the US had the same administrative efficiency as that of Canada, it would save $600 billion per year on administrative costs.

Most nations have relatively simple health insurance system. Usually there is a heavily government-regulated social insurance scheme covering 90 to 95 percent of the population, with uniform fee schedule and rules, and small private insurance market outside the social insurance scheme used by the upper income households. The US health system is highly complex, with myriad insurance schemes that vary by the socioeconomic and demographic status of the insured and by employer for families covered by employer-sponsored insurance (Reinhardt, 2019). Obviously, the private health insurance plans are unwieldy and messy, with huge inefficiencies and costs associated with them.

Unfettered Corporate Power

The health insurance industry today is dominated by a cartel of large, for-profit corporations. Some nonprofits that have remained are now behaving the same way to be able to compete with their for-profit counterparts (Potter, 2010). The health insurance industry scores more than 2,500 on the Herfindahl–Hirschman Index suggesting that it is highly concentrated (Nunn, Parsons, & Shambaugh, 2020). The high concentration in health care industry gives unfettered power to the member companies. Their practices geared to make more money have given rise to the numbers of uninsured and underinsured. Because of their corporate power, they resort to exploitative practices. They make promises they have no intention of keeping, flout regulations designed to protect consumers, make it nearly impossible to understand – or even obtain – information needed by consumers, routinely cancel the coverage of policy holders who get sick, and purge small businesses when their employees' medical claims exceed what underwriters expected (Potter, 2010).

Ryun (2018) argues that the American insurance companies are colluding with health care providers against the American people:

> We need to realize that health care providers and insurance companies have created a mutually beneficial racket. While on the surface it would appear they're competing, by the numbers, they're

actually not and have created a very beneficial system for themselves while sticking it to the American people. They are, in the
truest sense of word, colluding against the American people.

In support of his argument, he provides data on the performance of
stocks of health insurance companies from 2008 to 2018 in which the
health insurance companies outperformed S&P 500 from 2.5 times up to
5 times over nearly a decade. Between 2008 and 2018, while the S&P 500
saw 177 percent growth, the market value of the health insurance giant,
Aetna, went up by 445 percent, Humana by 608 percent, United Health
by 655 percent, and SIGNA by 866 percent. In 2017, United Health
Group, the nation's largest private health insurer, generated a revenue of
more than $200 billion with a gross profit margin of 24 percent.

Health insurers are in-charge of dispensing goods and ringing up
at the checkout (Zuger, 2017). They approve of some things and dis-
approve of others, as if on a whim. Even nonprofit Medicare and
Medicaid contract out services to some of these companies, whose first
responsibility is to their shareholders and profits. Their many tangled
and confusing plans and sub-plans have providers bouncing on and off
their rosters, destroying continuity of care and leaving the dreaded 'out
of network' charges behind. Similarly, medications move in and out of
approved drug lists depending on continual renegotiations between the
insurer and the manufacturer.

Ideally, private insurers and the Medicare should stop paying for
any medical treatments that unbiased experts agree provide no benefit
and may cause harm. Unfortunately, this is not the case in the health
care industry and many in the medical profession prefer not to apply
scientific evidence for the public's benefit because they (hospitals,
insurers, pharmaceuticals, and physicians) would lose income (Gibson
& Singh, 2010). In case of health care, incomes of health insurers rise
with increasing health care costs because their revenues are a percentage
of the total premiums, and their interest in curbing waste is therefore
lessened (Saini et al., 2017). Moreover, the behaviors of insurance
companies are subject to the distribution of power in the system – for
example, physicians, large hospital systems, pharmaceutical firms, and
medical device makers have a lot of say and insurance companies have
to coopt them. This cooptation has resulted into a fabricated system
that benefits all these system insiders at the expense of patients and the
overall society.

A report by the *Kaiser Family Foundation* (2018) compared the
increase in health care premiums with the increase in employee earnings
over three time periods. The report found that health care premiums

increased much faster than the employee earnings. Specifically, health care premiums increased by 78 percent from 2000 to 2006, 37 percent from 2006 to 2012, and 25 percent from 2012 to 2018 as compared to employee earnings of 20 percent, 18 percent, and 14 percent, respectively. The salaries of the executives of private health insurers keep going up. In 2009, WellPoint employed 39 executives who each earned a compensation exceeding $1 million annually. In contrast, the administrator, who managed 40 million Medicare and 59 million Medicaid members, received $176,000 a year (Potter, 2010).

Conclusion

The insurance companies have a history of undermining reform of the US health care system. They unleash a spin machine and run misinformation campaigns whenever there is a talk of reforming the system. The private health insurance with an expenditure of about $1.2 trillion accounts for the largest share of the total annual US health care spending of $3.8 trillion. It ranks #3 among all 83 industries in the US economy in the number of lobbyists and the amount spent on lobbying. Administrative complexity, because of the variety and complexity of private health insurance plans, amounts to an annual waste of $246 billion. Private health insurers have an unfettered power because of their role as both the sellers of insurance and the buyers of health care services. Health insurers now oversee physicians' work and decide which drugs and procedures receive coverage and compel physicians to follow the recommended treatment blueprints in exchange for reimbursements. Private health insurance market is highly concentrated that impedes competition, giving a handful of large insurers immense power.

References

Belk, D. 2018. Conclusion: How did we get here and why is this so hard to fix? http://truecostofhealthcare.org/wp-content/uploads/2018/11/Conclusion.pdf

Brownlee, S. & Saini, V. 2017. Corrupt health care practices drive up costs and fail patients. *Huff Post.* May 26.

Center for Responsive Politics. 2020. Opensecrets.org.

Chapin, C.F. 2017. *Ensuring America's health: The public creation of the corporate health care system.* Cambridge University Press: New York.

Gibson, R. & Singh, J.P. 2010. *The treatment trap: How the overuse of medical care is wrecking your health and what you can do to prevent it.* Ivan R. Dee: Chicago.

Himmelstein, D.U., Campbell, T., & Woolhandler, S. 2020. Health care administrative costs in the United States and Canada, 2017. *Annals of Internal Medicine*, 172(2): 134–142.

Kaiser Family Foundation. 2018. Employer health benefits: Summary findings. September 1.

Navarro, V. 2008. Why congress did not enact health care reform. In C. Harrington & C.L. Estes (eds.), *Health policy: Crisis and reform in the U.S. health care delivery system*, pp. 414–418, Fifth Edition. Jones and Bartlett Publishers: Sudbury, MA.

Nunn, R., Parsons, J., & Shambaugh, J. 2020. A dozen facts about the economics of the US health care system. *Brookings*. March 10. www.brookings.edu/research/a-dozen-facts-about-the-economics-of-the-u-s-health-care-system/

Potter, W. 2009. The health care industry vs health reform. http://wendellpotter.com/2009/06/the-health-care-industry-vs-health-reform/

Potter, W. 2010. *Deadly spin*. Bloomsbury Press: New York.

Quadagno, J. 2008. Why the United States has no national health insurance: Stakeholder mobilization against the welfare state, 1945–1996. In C. Harrington & C.L. Estes (eds.), *Health policy: Crisis and reform in the U.S. health care delivery system*, pp. 419–426, Fifth Edition. Jones and Bartlett Publishers: Sudbury, MA.

Reinhardt, U.E. 2019. *Priced out: The economic and ethical costs of American health care*. Princeton University Press: Princeton, NJ.

Ryun, N. 2018. Mr. President, End the Collusion…in the Healthcare Industry. *amgreatness.com*. April 28.

Saini, V., Garcia-Armesto, S., Klemperer, D., Paris, V., Elshaug, A.G., Brownlee, S., Ioannidis, J.P.A., & Fisher, E.S. 2017. Drivers of poor medical care. *Lancet,* 390: 178–190.

Shrank, W.H., Rogstad, T.L. & Parekh, N. 2019. Waste in the US health care system: estimated costs and potential savings. *JAMA*, 322(15): 1501–1509.

Zuger, A. 2017. Oh, Doctor: The profit-driven disaster that is U.S. health care. Book review of 'An American Sickness'. https://undark.org/2017/06/13/books-rosenthal-american-sickness/

7 Hospitals and Hospital Networks

The symptoms of a crony capitalistic system, such as unimaginative, unproductive, inefficient, and wasteful initiatives, programs, products, and services, are evident in US hospitals. Crony firms invest their fortunes in teams of lawyers, accountants, lobbyists, and political contributions to ensure that the system continues to work on their behalf (Salter, 2014). In 2019 alone, hospitals and nursing homes employed 807 lobbyists and spent $106 million on lobbying (*Center for Responsive Politics*, 2020) allowing them to merge with other hospitals without any antitrust violations, keep their pricing practices opaque, and bill facility fees in emergency room (ER) services and charge patients arbitrarily.

The business model of hospitals tilts toward making money by affecting the system through favorable health policy and legislation rather than making money by being efficient and producing high quality and innovative products and services (Khatri, Baveja, Boren, & Mammo, 2006; Khatri, Gupta, & Varma, 2017; Khatri, Pasupathy, & Hicks, 2012). In the last two to three decades, hospitals have focused more on mergers and acquisitions with the result that the hospital market in the US has become super concentrated allowing hospitals to charge higher prices because of reduced competition (Gale, 2015; Mathur, Srivastava, & Mehta, 2015). Hospitals in a super concentrated market can operate inefficiently and provide poor quality care, but still thrive.

The US hospitals lack a culture of innovation (Leifer, 2014). Not speaking as much of medical technologies, but the lack of creative and strategic thinking that could address the profound deficiencies in the current health care system. The health care providers lag behind other industries by a decade or more in their management practices. Failures of care delivery and coordination in health care settings – unnecessary admissions, avoidable complications, readmissions, lack of adoption of preventive care practices, clinician-related inefficiencies,

DOI: 10.4324/9781003112204-9

and hospital-acquired conditions and adverse events – because of poor organizing and management practices result in annual waste in the US health care system in the range of $130 billion to $244 billion (Shrank, Rogstad, & Parekh, 2019).

Among major health care players – such as the drug companies, private insurers, and physicians – hospitals have gotten an upper hand in recent years as their market position in the health care industry appears to have given them more leverage vis-à-vis other players in the industry. This can be inferred from the fact that hospitals' costs have now taken a center stage, growing more quickly than costs for other services, climbing about 15 percent over the last three years (Girod et al., 2020). The increase in the hospital cost by 4 percent each year for the last five years have been twice the rate of growth of the US gross domestic product. In the meantime, salaries of hospital administrators keep going up even when affordability, access, and quality of health care services suffer.

The rest of the chapter looks into how hospitals and hospital networks have contributed to the dysfunction in the US health care system.

Overuse of Medical Procedures and Services

Overuse of medical procedures and services is pervasive in the US hospitals and results in annual waste in the US health care system to the tune of $76 billion to $101 billion (Shrank, Rogstead, & Parekh, 2019). Although estimates vary, some experts believe that less than half of all medical care is based on adequate evidence about its effectiveness (Patashnik, Gerber, & Dowling, 2017).

Uninsured and underinsured Americans often get less testing and fewer services than they need. But well-insured Americans suffer often from too much treatment – particularly as they age. For example, people on the Medicare get more colonoscopies than guidelines recommend (Rosenthal, 2017). Colonoscopies performed for adults over the age of 75 are unlikely to benefit them as colon cancer progresses slowly (Rowan, 2013). Thus, early detection is less likely to benefit older adults since colonoscopies come with a risk of perforation of the intestine and bleeding.

Hospital administrators routinely urge ER personnel to meet quotas for admissions, whether or not patients actually need to be admitted to the hospital. Meanwhile, their billing offices have perfected the art of "upcoding", manipulating patient diagnoses in order to game payment systems and costing the Medicare an estimated $10 billion a year

(Brownlee & Saini, 2017). Hiring a large staff for billing and coding has become an important tool to maximize reimbursements.

Hospital administrators know that if their doctors bring in enough business – surgery, imaging, home-nursing referrals – they make money; and if they get the doctors bring in more, they make more (Gawande, 2009). Many hospitals tie salaries of physicians to relative value units (RVUs), sometimes offer 'productivity bonuses' based on them. Some hospitals even deduct money from salaries of doctors if their RVUs are too low. Rather than a fixed salary, compensation based on RVUs provides an incentive to physicians to prescribe more procedures. To overcome exactly this kind of unethical behavior from their physicians, Mayo Clinic uses salary-based compensation for its physicians rather than the traditional fee-for-service.

The Cost Conundrum: Two Different Models of Care

Gawande (2009) explains the cost conundrum in the US health care system by comparing the cost and quality of patient care provided by two hospitals using different models of care: McAllen, Texas and Mayo, Minnesota. McAllen in Hidalgo County has one of the lowest household incomes, but one of the most expensive health care in the country. In 2006, Medicare spending per enrollee in McAllen was about $15,000. Medicare spending in El Paso County in 2006 in the same state of Texas about 800 miles from McAllen with similar demographics (same percentage of non-English speakers, illegal immigrants, and unemployed and similar public health statistics) was only $7,500 per enrollee. The high cost of care in McAllen could not be attributed to better treatments or application of superior technologies because on all 25 but 2 metrics of care McAllen's hospitals performed worse than El Paso's. Gawande suggested that the main driver of McAllen's high costs was simply the across-the-board overuse of medicine. Compared with the patients in El Paso and nationwide, the patients in McAllen got significantly more diagnostic testing, hospital treatments, surgeries, and more home care.

While Americans may believe more care is better, research suggests that more medicine may be worse (Gawande, 2009). This is because nothing in medicine is without risk. In contrast to McAllen, the Mayo Clinic dominates the medical care in Rochester, Minnesota. It offers high quality of care using high levels of technological capability, but the Medicare spending is only $6,688 per enrollee, less than half of McAllen.

While physicians interviewed at McAllen hospitals attributed high costs of care there to 'culture of money', doctors are paid a fixed salary at Mayo Clinic and they spend as much time as a patient needs rather than shuttling patients in and out of rooms. The doctors and nurses, and even janitors, sit in meetings, work on ideas to make the services and care better. The focus is not on reimbursements. With less focus on revenue generation and more focus on the right kind of treatment, naturally the cost of patient care comes down and quality of patient care goes up.

Gawande terms the two contrasting models as a battle for the soul of American medicine. And he raises the question: Is the doctor set up to meet the needs of the patient first and foremost, or to maximize their and hospital's revenue? Paying doctors for quantity rather than for quality and paying them individually rather than as a member of the team working together for their patients explain the high cost of patient care with average clinical outcomes in the US.

The worrisome thing, according to Gawande, is that the Mayo model is losing. Many people in medicine do not see why they should do the hard work of organizing themselves in ways that reduce waste and improve quality if it means sacrificing revenue. Some of the doctors in well-organized hospitals using a similar model as Mayo Clinic have begun to complain about leaving the money on the table.

The Hospital Charge Master: An Exploitative Pricing Tool

A common billing tool that hospitals use is the hospital charge master that maintains a master list of charges (Leifer, 2014; Rosenthal, 2017). The funny thing is that no consideration is given to quality, safety, or outcome of the patient care when constructing the charge master. There seems to be no process, nor any rationale, behind the core document that is the basis for hundreds of billions of dollars in health care bills. There is no other industrialized nation hampered by the lack of true price transparency in the health care as the US. In countries such as Japan or the Netherlands or Israel, a national fee schedule is published that sets forth exactly what a doctor, therapist, or a hospital is paid for any treatment or medication.

The US hospitals use arcane terms to render the billing process of health care services virtually incomprehensible, deliberately so as there is profit in obfuscation (Leifer, 2014; Reinhardt, 2019). The process of health care procedures and services are kept trade secrets between insurers and providers of care. In large hospitals and hospital networks that have subsumed most of the American health care, no one on the front lines knows how much any of the billed items actually cost. Every health care system's price list for services provided is top secret, is likely to be inconsistent with the list of the network down the street, is based on crafty and confidential negotiation, and is often adjustable (Rosenthal, 2017).

Hospital administrators often evoke a default but false narrative that hospital must charge private insurers or patients without insurance more to make up for loss of revenue because of the lower Medicare reimbursements. The truth is that a hospital's market strength – not what Medicare pays – determines what a hospital is paid by private insurers (Potter, 2010).

Rosenthal (2017) terms hospitals as "sharks" or "spending machines". Hospitals charge patients who are uninsured or self-pay 2.5 times more than they charge those covered by health insurance and 3 times more than the amount allowed by the Medicare. The gap has grown considerably since the 1980s. Not-for-profit hospitals are now just as profitable as capitalist corporations, but the excess money they generate is not called 'profit' but 'operating surplus'.

The Coding as an Industry

Billing and coding of medical claims for reimbursement from Medicare by health care providers has spawned a "crazy industry" of coders (Rosenthal, 2017). It is endlessly complex, so that now there are coding degrees and coding specialists and profession of coding. The insurers have coders to make sure hospitals are coding correctly. The doctors learn coding so that they can make sure their office gets the money they deserve for what they have done.

Coders have contributed to higher costs for patients because salaries of this new layer of professionals and their years of education are reflected in the medical bills (Rosenthal, 2017). For example, the Duke University health system with 957 beds employs an army of billing clerks – 1,600 to be exact. A recent study estimated an annual health care waste owing to billing and coding termed as administrative complexity to the tune of $248 billion annually (Shrank, Rogstad, & Parekh, 2019).

Because, in the US, codes define not just disease states but also the procedures and treatments that the medical profession can sell, providers, insurers, and regulators lobby for and fight over each code rule and revision. Having your code as part of the lexicon matters (Rosenthal, 2017). Medical codes in the US are determined by a committee of the for-profit physicians' association, the American Medical Association. In Japan, the prices of various medical procedures and services are determined by a committee that has representatives from various segments of the society including members that represent the interests of citizens and experts from academia.

Super Concentration of Hospital Markets and Undermining of Competition

Hospitals have done everything in their power to create monopolies and avoid competition (Gale, 2015). Consequently, markets for both hospitals and physicians have become more concentrated. Consolidation of medical providers, barriers to market entry, and the closing of rural hospitals and private physician practices have resulted in market concentration, which allows providers to set higher prices without losing customers. A commonly used concentration metric is called the Herfindahl–Hirschman Index (HHI). The HHI has the following market concentration categories: unconcentrated (HHI < 1,500), moderately concentrated (1,500 ≤ HHI < 2,500), highly concentrated (2,500 ≤ HHI < 5,000), and super concentrated (HHI ≥ 5,000). Hospitals, specialist physicians, and insurers are all above the threshold of 2,500 for high concentration, with hospital concentration especially high with an HHI of 5,790 in 2016, qualifying it as a super concentrated market (Nunn, Parsons, & Shambaugh, 2020).

The health care provider concentration has buffeted American health care system in the last three decades (Starr, 2017). Hospitals have integrated not only horizontally by merging with other hospitals but also vertically by buying practice groups such as radiologists, surgical units, skilled nursing facilities, and home health providers. These developments followed the weakening of antitrust and merger regulations at the state and federal level, which were facilitated by changes in academic and legal doctrine (Starr, 2017). The number of physicians in private practice and the number of private practices have declined since 2000 (Mathur, Srivastava, & Mehta, 2015). In 2005, more than two-thirds of the medicine practices were owned by physicians; in 2010, only 35 percent of the physicians were practicing independently. This is mainly due to large hospital-based health care systems taking over physicians' practices. From 1998 to 2012, about 5,000 hospitals in the US saw 1,133 mergers and acquisitions (Salam, 2015).

The major effect of consolidation is simply a significant rise in prices because hospital conglomerates that have driven out competition can raise prices without losing any patients. The existence of one dominant health care system in a region can result in price increase as high as 40 to 50 percent (Xu, Wu, & Makary, 2015). Hospital mergers have been found to have more cardiac procedures and an increase in inpatient deaths indicating suboptimal care and overtreatment (Rosenthal, 2017). The rates of mortality and health care quality problems have been shown to increase when competition falls (Frakt, 2018).

There is no empirical support for the claims that mergers harness economies of scale and scope. On the contrary, the health care industry is an exception in that it defies the logic of the economics of scale. The cost of care goes up and the quality of care comes down as the size of a hospital increases (Khatri, Gupta, & Varma, 2017). This happens because health care organizations, especially hospitals, are poorly organized and managed. Thus, as the size of a health care organization increases, the operations become more fragmented and messier, resulting in lower organizational performance both in terms of cost and quality (Khatri, Pasupathy, & Hicks, 2012).

To make things worse, Medicare pays hospitals more than other sites of service for the same medical procedures on the grounds that hospitals perform several unique and valuable functions, like providing uncompensated care. Unsurprisingly, hospitals are buying physician practices as fast as they can to capture patient procedures and diagnostics for which they are paid in multiples of what independent physicians are paid. For example, in New Jersey, a hotbed of independent physician practice sellouts, cardiologists receive $850 for an in-office nuclear stress test while hospitals get about $5,000 for the same test performed by the same physician (Doulgeris, 2014).

Surprise Billing

A well-functioning market offers price transparency. Consumers can compare price and quality differences among different options. The US health care market fails to meet this standard. Erma Bombeck, American humorist, aptly notes about hospitals: Getting out of the hospital is a lot like resigning from a book club and you are not out of it until the computer says you are out of it. One common practice that hospitals resort to is called 'surprise billing', when insured patients find out, after receiving health care services at an in-network facility, that the provider (e.g., the surgeon in the emergency department) was outside of their insurance network. This increases the costs for patients and allows providers to charge higher prices than those that were negotiated by insurers, raising overall costs. The surprise billing is common when patients use ambulance services or visit emergency department, but it occurs even when receiving elective hospital care. Surprise billing in emergencies presents special problems to patients and their families as they have little or no ability to compare prices and choose the best option. The medical practitioners in anesthesiology, emergency medicine, diagnostic radiology, and pathology charge multiples of amount allowed by the Medicare (Nunn, Parsons, & Shambaugh, 2020). Mean charges for emergency medicine are as much as 5.4 times higher than the Medicare rate.

The Emergency Room Services

The health care providers have turned ER services into a new cash cow. There are millions of ER visits every year, making it one of the more frequent ways patients interact with the health care system. Because of frequent complaints and reports of malfeasance in billing of ER services, Kliff (2018) asked Vox readers to submit ER bills over a period of 15 months. She received 1,182 bills and found, among other things, hospitals were charging outrageous facility fees as part of services provided in ER. The facility fee, the charge for walking through an ER's doors, could range from $533 to $3,000. The prices were high, even for things that one can buy in a drugstore. For example, eye drops of a generic drug called ofloxacin cost as much as $238 in an emergency department in a hospital, whereas a vial of this drug can be purchased at a retail pharmacy for $25. Cost of a Tylenol tablet in a hospital setting may be billed as high as $25. A simple pregnancy test in a hospital costs $236 in Texas, $147 in Illinois, $111 in California, and $465 in Georgia. Patients, who after researching and making sure that they are going to an in-network hospital, ended up with big bills because they went to an in-network hospital but were seen by an out-of-network doctor. Patients were charged just for sitting in a waiting room and faced steep bills even if they did not see a doctor. Despite not receiving any treatment, they ended up with a hefty fee because of the facility fee.

Collusion between Hospitals and Insurance Companies

Making health care expensive benefits both the hospitals and the insurers (Belk, 2018). It is well-established that the hospital bills have excessive markups. While overbilling drives up health care costs, it also serves to strengthen the power insurance companies have on health care. Since insurance companies never have to pay the insanely high billing charges that hospitals and other health care providers use, these billing charges allow the health insurance companies to act as protection rackets. Patients need health insurance to 'protect' them from $80,000 hospital bill, even though the insurance company might only pay $15,000 for that bill.

Lab Tests and Ancillary Services such as Physical Therapy

Over the course of the past decade, lab tests and ancillary services have become to hospitals and clinics what booze is to restaurants: high-profit margin items that can be billed for nearly any amount (Rosenthal, 2017). Better still, many insurers require no co-pay for these items once patients have met their deductibles; therefore, most patients avail these services anyway, whether needed or not, as they have not to pay for them.

Thanks largely to the lobbying efforts of the American Physical Therapy Association, a physical therapy consultation has become a precondition of nearly every hospital discharge (Rosenthal, 2017). Many of these therapy consultations and prescriptions seem problematic in terms of evidence-based medicine. But that does not matter. The US physical and occupational therapy industry was worth $34.5 billion in 2018, up from $26.2 billion in 2014. The total market is forecast to grow at about 6.2 percent annually.

Hospital-induced Injuries, Illnesses, and Deaths

Hospital-induced injuries, illnesses, and deaths are a major problem in the US. In the automotive industry, there are extensive warranties on the product in order to provide a safeguard to individuals purchasing the product. In health care, not only there are no warranties, but providers stand to profit from the problems they create through poor quality delivery. For example, Leifer (2014; p.145) based on his consultancy experience noted:

> More than once I encountered hospital executives who explained that the errors that I wanted to help them eliminate contributed to their hospital's bottom line. In speaking with consultants, I realized that such discussions were happening quietly in executive conference rooms across America.

Cozy Relationships between Hospitals and Local TV Stations

Gibson and Singh (2010) report cozy relationships between hospitals and local television stations. Viewers who think they are getting news are really getting a form of advertising. Local stations across the country are less likely to report on medical mistakes or hospital-acquired infections because of this cliquish relationship. An epidemic of fake health care news is blurring the line between news and advertising. On the other hand, there is usually a segment in local news almost daily extolling a miracle drug, or treatment, or a procedure. Doing so keeps feeding the narrative of great innovations and advancements in the US health care system.

Conclusion

US hospitals are the poster boys of crony capitalism. Crony firms invest their vast fortunes in teams of lawyers, accountants, lobbyists, and political contributions to ensure that the system continues to work on their behalf. This is the approach large hospitals and hospital networks have employed. US hospitals have lacked a culture of innovation and creative and strategic thinking that would address the profound deficiencies in today's health care system. Instead, they have shown their adeptness in devising newer and better rent seeking strategies. The hospital markets in the US are super concentrated giving hospitals monopoly power in pricing of their products and services. Hospitals are well-known for opaqueness in pricing. They use the hospital charge master as a pricing tool, which is an arbitrary, exploitative tool. Hospitals devise new ways of milking the system such as lab tests and ancillary services, surprise billing, and ER services. Hospitals rely on overtreatments of medical procedures and services to enhance their revenues that cost taxpayers $76 billion to $101 billion annually. Poor organization and management of health care providers in the form of failures of care delivery and coordination while adds to their revenues costs taxpayers in the range of $177 billion to $243 billion annually. As a barometer of where the current US health care system stands, the Mayo Clinic model offering a well-organized, cost-effective, and high-quality care is losing out to the McAllen model, which is generating more revenues despite offering average or substandard patient care because it gets reimbursed more for its inefficiencies and overtreatments. What a system!

References

Belk, D. 2018. Conclusion: How did we get here and why is this so hard to fix? http://truecostofhealthcare.org/wp-content/uploads/2018/11/Conclusion.pdf

Brownlee, S. & Saini, V. 2017. Corrupt health care practices drive up costs and fail patients. *Huff Post.* May 26.

Center for Responsive Politics. 2020. Opensecrets.org.

Doulgeris, J. 2014. Healthcare's perfect storm of greed and incompetence. *Physicians Practice.* October 16.

Frakt, A. 2018. Medical mystery: Something happened to US health spending after 1980. *New York Times,* May 14.

Gale, A.H. 2015. Bigger but not better: Hospital mergers increase costs and do not improve quality. *Missouri Medicine*, 112(1): 4–5.

Gawande, A. 2009. The cost conundrum. *The New Yorker.* June 1.

Gibson, R. & Singh, J.P. 2010. *The treatment trap: How the overuse of medical care is wrecking your health and what you can do to prevent it.* Ivan R. Dee: Chicago.

Girod, C.S., Houchens, P.R., Liner, D.M., Naugle, A.L., Norris, D., & Weltz, S.A. 2020. 2020 Milliman Index. https://us.milliman.com/en/insight/2020-milliman-medical-index

Khatri, N., Baveja, A., Boren, S., & Mammo, A. 2006. Medical errors and quality of care: From control to commitment. *California Management Review*, 48(3): 115–141.

Khatri, N., Gupta, V., & Varma, A. 2017. The relationship between HR capabilities and quality of patient care: The mediating role of proactive work behaviors. *Human Resource Management*, 56(4), 673–691.

Khatri, N., Pasupathy, K.S., & Hicks, L.L. 2012. The crucial role of people and information in health care organizations. In G.D. Brown, K.S. Pasupathy, & T. Patrick (eds.), *Health informatics: Transforming health care*, pp. 197–212. Health Administration Press: Chicago.

Kliff. S. 2018. I read 1,182 emergency room bills this year. Here's what I learned. *Vox.* December 18.

Leifer, J. 2014. *The myth of modern medicine: The alarming truth about American health care.* Rowman & Littlefield: Lanham, MD.

Mathur, P., Srivastava, S., & Mehta, J.L. 2015. High cost of healthcare in the United States: A manifestation of corporate greed. *Journal of Forensic Medicine*, 1: 1.

Nunn, R., Parsons, J., & Shambaugh, J. 2020. A dozen facts about the economics of the US health care system. *Brookings.* March 10. www.brookings.edu/research/a-dozen-facts-about-the-economics-of-the-u-s-health-care-system/

Patashnik, E.M., Gerber, A.S., & Dowling, C.M. 2017. *Unhealthy politics: The battle over evidence-based medicine.* Princeton University Press: Princeton and Oxford.

Potter, W. 2010. *Deadly spin.* Bloomsbury Press: New York.

Reinhardt, U.E. 2019. *Priced out: The economic and ethical costs of American health care.* Princeton University Press: Princeton, NJ.

Rosenthal, E. 2017. *An American sickness: How healthcare became a big business and how you can take it back.* Penguin Press: New York.

Rowan, K. 2013. Scientific American. Many colonoscopies for seniors carry unnecessary risks. March 12. www.scientificamerican.com/article/many-colonoscopies-for-seniors-carry-unnecessary-risks/

Salam, R. 2015. Hospitals are robbing us blind. *Slate.* March 24.

Salter, M.S. 2014. *Crony capitalism, American style: what are we talking about here?* Working Paper 15-025. Edmund J. Safra Center for Ethics, Harvard University: Boston, MA.

Shrank, W.H., Rogstad, T.L., & Parekh, N. 2019. Waste in the US health care system: Estimated costs and potential savings. *JAMA*, 322(15): 1501–1509.

Starr, P. 2017. *The social transformation of American medicine: The rise of sovereign profession and the making of a vast industry* (2nd edition). Basic Books: New York.

Xu, T., Wu, A.W., & Makary, M.A. 2015. The potential hazards of hospital consolidation: Implications for quality, access, and price. *Journal of Medical Association*, 314: 1337–1338.

8 Physicians

American Medical Association (AMA) played a crucial role in making of the US health care system that exists today. While its role at present may have diminished because of the emergence of other specialty medical societies and other more powerful players such as private health insurers, pharmaceutical companies, and hospitals, it trailblazed the health care policy in the early 20th century. It developed a sophisticated approach to affect health policies by lobbying influential politicians and relevant political committees. It developed a powerful alliance with private health insurers to defeat efforts to reform the US health care system by national leaders on several occasions.

As health care system has become large and complex, many interest groups within the medical profession itself have emerged. One thing that seems common is that many of these interest groups have followed the AMA footprints. Some of these interest groups (medical societies) have formed super political action committees (PACs) that allow these medical specialties pursue their interest in a more direct and focused manner. Specialty medical societies are rich and some of the specialty PACs now spend more on lobbying than the AMA Super PAC (AMPAC). The prominent specialty medical societies with their own Super PACs include ACC PAC (Cardiologists), BrainPAC (Neurologists), FamMedPAC (Family Medicine), NEMPAC (Emergency Medicine), Orthopedic PAC, RADPAC (Radiologists), and SkinPAC (Dermatology).

For the past 80 years or so, physicians and their allies have lobbied legislators, cultivated sympathetic candidates through large campaign contributions, organized petition drives, created grassroots protests, and developed new "products" whenever government action seemed imminent (Quadagno, 2008). Altogether physicians/medical professionals employed 796 lobbyists and spent $97 million in lobbying in 2019 (*Center for Responsive Politics*, 2020), ranking them #12 out of 83 industries in the US economy. Physicians still have much sway on health policy, but

DOI: 10.4324/9781003112204-10

other big players – pharmaceutical firms, private health insurers, and hospitals – may have become more powerful than physicians because of the financial resources these other players have, and thus diluting some of the hegemony that physicians once enjoyed.

The composition of the anti-reform coalition has evolved, dominated first by physicians, with health insurers moving to the forefront of the resistance to reform as physicians' antipathy to national health insurance has dwindled – tempered by the benefits of guaranteed payment, split among various specialty groups, and loss of allies among other health professionals and employer groups (Quadagno, 2008).

This chapter lays out how physicians have contributed to the current US health care system dysfunction.

The Company Insurance Model

The company insurance model means that the company or the employer offers health insurance for their employees. The medical profession of the early 20th century, working through AMA, played a significant role in forming the early building blocks of the US health care system. One mantra that physicians through AMA have pursued is that no matter how the system be organized, the government control had to stay out of it. This way a physician's practice would not be dictated by the government. At the same time, physicians have wanted to have a reliable, trouble-free payment mechanism for the care they provide, and thus was born the company insurance model, which remains its main feature (Belk, 2018; Chapin, 2017). Third-party insurers, AMA concluded, offered the best hope of preserving the traditional model for delivering health care via individual practitioners.

The AMA's opposition to Truman and his proposal of nationalized health insurance program, and its successful partnership with private health insurers, put into motion the market forces that eventually took control of American health care (Potter, 2010).

This basic company insurance model pursued by AMA in alliance with private insurers has weathered many attempts by politicians to reform it. Unfortunately, AMA's venture does not seem to have turned out as well as it had hoped. The US health care system dysfunction that we see today could be attributed significantly to this model. The AMA's strategy has had a major unintended consequence that became apparent over time. The company insurance model evolved to weaken the position of doctors while endowing private health insurers more power over health care. Health insurers now oversee physicians' work and decide which drugs and procedures receive coverage and compel physicians to follow treatment blueprints in exchange for reimbursements. If insurance companies refuse to cover a medical procedure, it might as well not exist.

The Fee-for-Service Model

The fee-for-service model has contributed greatly to the US health care system dysfunction. In contrast with fixed salaries for physicians (e.g., Mayo Clinic), fee-for-service encourages greed and unethical behavior because by doing more tests and procedures everybody in the system makes more money (Mathur, Srivastava, & Mehta, 2015). The system of payment influences the behavior of health care professionals far more than the standards of professionalism promulgated in the code of ethics (Saini et al., 2017).

The fee-for-service undermines value for patients and has held back improvements in the quality of care and led to escalating costs (Porter & Kaplan, 2016). It does so in number of ways. First, fee-for-service rewards providers for poor outcomes. Since providers are reimbursed based on the volume of care, they make more money not just for performing unnecessary services but for poor outcomes too as complications result in additional services for which providers get reimbursed again. It is no accident that there is an epidemic of overtreatment in the US health care system (Gibson & Singh, 2010; Leifer, 2014; Patashnik, Gerber, & Dowling, 2017; Rosenthal, 2017). Overtreatments account for annual waste in the US health care system ranging between $76 billion and $101 billion (Shrank, Rogstad, & Parekh, 2019).

Second, fee-for-service furthers duplication and lack of coordination. Under fee-for-service, providers receive payments for individual procedures and services, rather than for the treatment of a patient's condition over the entire care cycle. In response, providers have organized around functional specialties and multiple independent providers are involved in each patient's treatment, resulting in poorly coordinated care, duplicated services, and no accountability for health outcomes. Unnecessary admissions, avoidable complications, and readmissions contribute the annual waste in the system in the range of $27 billion to $78 billion (Shrank, Rogstad, & Parekh, 2019).

Third, fee-for-service perpetuates inefficiency. As discussed under the cost conundrum in Chapter 7, health care providers with poor quality of care (e.g., McAllen, Texas) get reimbursed twice the amount of good quality care providers (e.g., Mayo Clinic, Minnesota). Inefficient providers not only survive but thrive despite high costs and poor outcomes (Gawande, 2009).

Physicians, who own a share in the testing facility or equipment, have been found to refer patients for unnecessary imaging tests such as CT and MRI scans (Brownlee & Saini, 2017). In general, there is constant pressure on physicians to increase billing for the services provided to patients by hospital administration. An increase in the services provided at each visit and scheduling multiple visits for the same or related problems enhance the hospital revenue (Mathur, Srivastava, & Mehta, 2015).

Physicians in the US do not like the single payer/universal system that all other developed and developing countries have adopted because such a system renders control of pricing health care services in the hands of the federal government just like other countries. Physicians in the US also do not like patients to pay out of pocket because that would bring market forces into play. The current fragmented system is serving physicians' financial interests rather well and they would like to keep it intact. The current system suffers from the problem of "other people's money" (Herzlinger, 2018). Often a patient ordering and receiving medical care mistakenly believes he or she is not the one paying for it.

The chief concern of physicians is always about the reimbursement rates for the medical procedures and services that they provide. Physicians are particular about what they are paid for their every minute and procedure. The system has become such that a patient get charged even if the doctor only says, hi, how are you doing, see you later (Solman, 2017).

A study on how physicians lobby their members of Congress found that physicians frequently lobbied members of the Congress and estimated that about 20,000 meetings took place annually between the physicians and the health legislative assistants (Landers & Sehgal, 2000). The most common issues physicians discussed with legislators included reimbursement, managed care reform, and medical research funding. By contrast, other issues such as access to care for uninsured citizens, cost of health care, tobacco control, abortion rights, and gun violence were rarely brought up by physician lobbyists. It seems that the issues that physicians lobby about are different from the health care issues that voters want the Congress to address. Physicians have parlayed their professional expertise into amassing legal, institutional, and economic power for the profession, but have not asserted this power to reform the health care system (Quadagno, 2008).

Physicians and their allies have a long, trailblazing history of lobbying legislators, cultivating sympathetic candidates through large campaign contributions, organizing petition drives, creating grassroots protests, and developing new "products" that strengthen their grip on the system (Quadagno, 2008).

The Biomedical Model

The prevalent biomedical model of health care in the US focuses on biological factors and excludes psychological, environmental, and social influences. This model does not consider individual's lifestyle or their environment, both of which play a major role in the physical and mental wellness of individuals. The single-minded focus in the biomedical model is on treating patients after they get sick. Prevention as a source of good health of individuals does not receive adequate attention. There are clear consequences of doing so. The US is a chronically ill nation and ranks high in poor lifestyle choices by its citizens that eventually catch up and take a major toll on their health and wellbeing. The system can make more money when people are sick rather than when they are healthy; preventive care may not be rewarding financially. Other developed nations spend about twice as much on public health as they spend on medical care, which is the opposite of what the US does. The US spends about twice as much on medical care than public health.

The biomedical model, flawed for not considering the experiential and cultural aspects of medical care, moved more in the direction of a business model than toward an anthropological one as medical practice became fully enmeshed in the burgeoning trillion dollars for-profit industry (Eiser, 2014).

The Breakdown of Basic Ethics, Hippocratic Oath

A commonly held belief is that the health care professionals are into health care because of their calling, they want to serve the sick and indigent. There is no systematic study or evidence in support of such a belief. On the contrary, a study found that those selected for medical school are not so empathetic and that the medical school and medical education tend to reduce empathy in residents (Lown et al., 2007). Other studies report decline of emotional intelligence during medical school (Wagner et al., 2005) and decline in empathy during residency training (Bellinin & Shea, 2005).

When it comes to the reports of unethical behavior on the part of physicians, the usual explanation advanced is that there are a few bad apples. It seems that the examples of a few bad apples that we hear in the news are the ones that get reported because they are too egregious.

Many others do not get reported. However, the way the system has evolved over time and a closer look at the unscrupulous behavior in health care, both of the above explanations – calling and a few bad apples – seem insufficient to explain the greed and waste that we see in the system. Much more convincing explanation of the symptoms of the problem that we see in the US health care system is that of crony capitalism or greed or institutionalized corruption (English, 2013; Gibson & Singh, 2010; Rosenthal, 2017). Rather than a few bad apples, the greed and resulting unethical behavior are ubiquitous in the health care industry. Physicians who bring in more money by overprescribing procedures get rewarded handsomely and accorded the status of a star in the system (Leifer, 2014).

Physicians think about money a lot – about how to increase their incomes, about the cost of running their offices, about what their colleagues in other specialties make, about what plumbers make for house calls, and what a liquor dealer's net is compared to their own (Millenson, 2015). A quote by a physician as reported by Gibson and Singh (2010) is quite telling:

> About ten years ago there used to be a few people doing bad medicine for money. Now doing bad medicine for money has become institutionalized. The economic machine is grinding people up for money ... Every week cases are done at this hospital that shouldn't be done.

Greed becomes a sin when it threatens to compromise the provision of appropriate care. Leifer (2014; p.18) notes:

> Once driven by a combination of altruism and a fervor for harnessing scientific knowledge for the benefit of the society, medicine has been increasingly replaced by greed. This factor is the most insidious of all and applies not only to a segment of the physician population but too many other stakeholders within the health care delivery system.

Physicians and Conflicts of Interest

The relationship between doctors and commercial interests is woven deeply into the fabric of medicine (Rogers, 2007). Even though only about 20 percent of all medical spending goes toward physicians' services, physicians determine most of the total spending (Henderson, 2012). Physicians prescribe the drugs, admit patients into the hospitals, and order the tests. Principal agent theory is applicable in such a situation. An agency relationship exists where an individual – the principal (e.g., patient) – gives someone else – the agent (physician) – authority to make decisions on their behalf (Henderson, 2012). Problem arises when the interests of the principal (patient) and the agent (physician) diverge. In medicine, patients are relatively uninformed concerning alternative diagnoses and treatments. Further, when individuals visit a doctor, they are sick and consequently more vulnerable psychologically than healthy individuals. They end up deferring to and trusting physicians to make choices for them because of the difficulty in gathering and understanding medical information and being more vulnerable psychologically because of illness. In the absence of a physician being highly ethical, a physician's role can create a conflict of interest. Given this unique position, physicians can serve as imperfect agents, serving their own interests over those of their patients. Bradley and Taylor (2013) suggest that physicians overtreat patients based on financial incentives and patients agree to their treatment plan due to lack of medical knowledge and deference to authority.

Despite significant literature showing how physician integrity is susceptible to pharmaceutical and device manufacturers, the medical profession continues to allow them to have a detrimental influence on the practice of medicine and on physician respectability (Lichter, 2008). Pharmaceutical and device manufacturers exploit the continuing medical education programs to subtly 'buy' physicians one at a time allowing these companies to then influence physicians' and medical professionals' decisions on what drugs and devices they recommend.

Huntoon (2018), a physician and a member of the Association of American Physicians and Surgeons and editor-in-chief of the *Journal of American Physicians and Surgeons*, opines that the US medical industry is rife with conflicts of interest that lead to rampant corruption in prescriptions of procedures and treatments. As an example, he noted that pharmaceutical companies that produce medications for treating chronic obstructive pulmonary disease are prominently featured as the source of payments to board members who develop the guidelines on what medications to take.

Many specialty societies accept support from the industry and have become financially dependent to a considerable degree (Saini et al., 2017). Continuing medical education systems are funded largely by the industry, creating conflicts of interest that bias educational content. Other effective means to influence physicians' practice are sales representatives, distribution of drug samples, and journal advertising. These tactics tend to promote the use of more expensive brands over generics, often directly subverting practice guidelines and formulary policies. In 2010, 80 to 90 percent of marketing costs by PhRMA (Pharmaceutical Research and Manufacturers of America) were aimed at physicians, amounting to $23 billion into physicians' pockets (Leifer, 2014). Physicians often argue that the gifts or payments pose no conflict of interest because they have no effect on their practice patterns.

Gifts, free samples, travel subsidies, and entertainment are designed to create a sense of reciprocation. Research shows that industry–doctor interaction correlates with doctors' preferences for new products that hold no demonstrated advantage over existing ones, with decreased prescribing of more cost-effective generic drugs and increased and widespread prescribing of newer, invariably more expensive treatments.

In addition to higher costs, there are other downsides of the cozy relationships between commercial interest and medicine (Rogers, 2007). First, there is a potential damage to the doctor–patient relationship via undermining of the ethical principle of beneficence. The commitment by practitioners to act in their patients' best interest is necessary for good patient care and patients need to be able to trust their doctor's recommendation for treatment without concern about other pressures on the doctor's fidelity. A second harm concerns the moral character of doctors. There are numerous virtues traditionally ascribed to doctors – honesty, integrity, or fidelity. Engaging in relationships that create conflicts of interest may be quite damaging to these virtues, irrespective of a doctor's awareness of the consequences of the relationship.

Who Sets the Price for Medical Procedures and Treatments?

The cost of health care is not regulated by the government or a body representative of the interests of the overall society. Instead, prices are set by the Specialty Society Relative Value Scale Update Committee of the AMA. This committee consists of physicians representing various medical specialties. Three times a year the Relative Value Scale Update Committee meets to adjust the value of codes. The Medicare assigned the task of establishing codes and prices for various procedures and treatments to AMA. Such an arrangement in a capitalistic system is not a sound practice as it gives the entire control to private professional interests for pricing the medical procedures and services. The elaborate codes enable physicians to assign as much value as they want and cover whatever procedures and treatments they want.

Medical Malpractice Tort a Convenient Excuse for Defensive Medicine (Overtreatments)?

One common argument to explain the incidence of unnecessary health care services in the US is that physicians need to practice safe medicine to protect themselves from malpractice liability suits. Thus, there is a need for medical malpractice tort reform. Both the experts and laymen find this argument persuasive. I have believed in this argument for a longtime myself. However, as I understand the US health care system more deeply, I find this argument somewhat problematic. If physicians had *really* wanted a tort reform, given their political influence, they could have had it done long time ago. My view is that, for physicians and hospitals, medical malpractice tort offers a convenient excuse for defensive medicine. They have come to realize that the current medical malpractice tort is a boon for their business. Reforming the medical malpractice laws would take away one good excuse from them for overuse of clinical treatments and procedures. For example, a study that examined the net effects of medical malpractice tort reform on health insurance losses in Texas found that, unless physicians are otherwise penalized for providing unnecessary services, they are reluctant to reduce the income associated with these services, even if providers have reduced expected liability (Born, Karl, & Viscusi, 2017).

Physicians Blame the System and Other Players in the System

There is a bizarre martyr complex that permeates medicine – physicians and other medical professionals think they are working harder and longer for less money than everyone else in the US (Rosenthal, 2017). Doctors usually complain about other players in the US health care system, especially, the insurance companies without realizing that various professional bodies of physicians are one of the key players in formulating the health policies including what procedures are to be covered by insurance and how much rate to be charged for each procedure. Girgis (2015), a doctor, wrote a letter to the editor of *Physicians' Weekly* lamenting that her patients were suffering because they could not afford the premiums or the high deductibles. She further noted that she was seeing more diagnostic tests and procedures being denied by insurance and spent many hours a week fighting these denials. Her patients were suffering from bad medical consequences because they could not afford to get the medical care that they needed. What Girgis is forgetting is who is responsible for such a system and what physicians, who feel the victims of the system, are doing about it.

Another physician, London (2017) lays the blame squarely at doorsteps of insurance companies, pharmaceutical companies, and other large entities seeking to make money in medicine. She suggests physicians are not to be blamed as they account for only 20 percent of the spending in health care. She also warns that government, public, and other health care players need to stop squeezing physicians, giving them unfunded mandates, driving them out of the profession by making them miserable, and doubting their training.

Physicians argue that medicine is under threat from lawmakers, regulators, insurance companies, and hospital administrators and express deep frustrations and fears for their colleagues across the country who are experiencing unprecedented emotional and physical strain created by the dysfunctional system. While these physicians may be right in suggesting that the US health care system has become toxic, but they are wrong in blaming all other players except themselves for the problems in the system. Physicians are at the core of the health care system. They, through AMA and many other physicians' associations, are responsible to a great extent for the US health care system that exists today, especially its basic building blocks. Despite their position as a repository of public trust, doctors and their professional societies have not used their authority, standing, and prestige to promote the steps necessary to root out waste, bad science, and inefficiencies in the health care system – and too often have used their political capital to fight measures to reform the health care system (Patashnik, Gerber, & Dowling, 2017; Rosenthal, 2017).

The Malfunctioning Social Contract between Medical Profession and Society

The social contract between the medical profession and society is malfunctioning, and by all accounts, the failure of physicians to practice evidence-based medicine is a serious problem in the US (Patashnik, Gerber, & Dowling, 2017). The misuse of professional authority has undermined the efforts to tackle the medical evidence problem and curb wasteful spending (Frangioni, 2008).

Past federal efforts to promote evidence-based practices through medical research and clinical guideline development have crumbled under pressure from doctors, drug companies, and medical device makers as these groups profit from expensive but ineffective products, and thus have a lot to lose (Brownlee & Saini, 2017; Millenson, 2015; Gibson & Singh, 2010). Too much authority seems to be vested with the medical profession, partly because it is often impossible for patients to know what treatments are needed and effective, which in turn is partly due to general societal failure to recognize that the primary function of medical societies is to protect the autonomy and advance the interests of their members (Patashnik, Gerber, & Dowling, 2017).

Conclusion

Physicians themselves and the larger American public see physicians as innocent bystanders of the current crisis in the US health care system. The arguments laid out in this chapter suggest that such a belief is not well founded. Physicians are the key architects of the US health care system that exist today. The company insurance model, fee-for-service, and the biomedical model that lie at the core of the US health care system dysfunction could all be attributed to the lobbying efforts of AMA. Physicians/medical professionals are the fourth largest spender on lobbying among 83 industrial sectors in the US economy. Physicians form the core of any health care system as all health care necessarily runs through them and the decisions they make (Gawande, 2009). They have played a central role in structuring the US health care system that exists today. If it is dysfunctional, they need to accept at least part of the blame. Physicians tend to complain about the system that they have helped create but feel as if they are outsiders. Physicians are still resistant to change and are one of the most formidable hurdles in reforming the US health care system.

References

Belk, D. 2018. Conclusion: How did we get here and why is this so hard to fix? http://truecostofhealthcare.org/wp-content/uploads/2018/11/Conclusion. pdf

Bellinin, L.M. & Shea, J.M. 2005. Mood change and empathy decline persist during three years of medicine training. *Academic Medicine*, 80: 164–167.

Born, P.H., Karl, J.B., & Viscusi, W. 2017. The net effects of medical malpractice tort reform on health insurance losses: The Texas experience. *Health Economics Review*, 7: 1.

Bradley, E.H. & Taylor, L.A. 2013. *The American health care paradox: Why spending more is getting us less.* Public Affairs: New York.

Brownlee, S. & Saini, V. 2017. Corrupt health care practices drive up costs and fail patients. *Huff Post.* May 26.

Center for Responsive Politics. 2020. Opensecrets.org.

Chapin, C.F. 2017. *Ensuring America's health: The public creation of the corporate health care system.* Cambridge University Press: New York.

Eiser, A.R. 2014. *The ethos of medicine in postmodern America*. Lexington Books: Lanham, MD.

English, W. 2013. *Institutional corruption and the crisis of liberal democracy*. Working Paper No. 15. Edmond J. Safra Center for Ethics. Harvard University: Boston, MA.

Frangioni, J.V. 2008. The impact of greed on academic medicine and patient care. *Nature Biotechnology*, 26: 503–507.

Gawande, A. 2009. The cost conundrum. *The New Yorker*. June 1.

Gibson, R. & Singh, J.P. 2010. *The treatment trap: How the overuse of medical care is wrecking your health and what you can do to prevent it*. Ivan R. Dee: Chicago.

Girgis, L. 2015. Doctor's voice. Will corporate greed destroy our healthcare system? *Physician's Weekly*. January 23.

Henderson, J.W. 2012. *Health economics and policy*. Fifth Edition. South-Western: Mason, OH.

Herzlinger, R. 2018. The IRS can save American health care. *The Wall Street Journal*. July 1.

Huntoon, L. 2018. From the president corruption in medicine. *Journal of American Physicians and Surgeons*, 23(4): 102–104.

Landers, S.H. & Sehgal, A.R. 2000. How do physicians lobby their members of Congress? *Archives of Internal Medicine*, 160: 3248–3251.

Leifer, J. 2014. *The myth of modern medicine: The alarming truth about American health Care*. Rowman & Littlefield: Lanham, MD.

Lichter, P.R. 2008. CME, physicians, and Pavlov: Can we change what happens when industry rings the bell? *Transactions of the American Ophthalmological Society*, 106: 39–45.

London, C. 2017. A physician based in Maine. It's insurance companies, not Obamacare, that's making healthcare sick. *Opinion*. The Hill, July 12.

Lown, B.A., Chou, C.L., Clark, W.D. et al. 2007. Caring attitudes in medical education: Perceptions of deans and curriculum leaders. *Journal of General Internal Medicine*, 22(11): 1514–1522.

Mathur, P., Srivastava, S., & Mehta, J.L. 2015. High cost of healthcare in the United States: A manifestation of corporate greed. *Journal of Forensic Medicine*, 1: 1.

Millenson, M. 2015. The AMA's forgotten fight against physician greed. *The Health Care Blog*. September 10.

Patashnik, E.M., Gerber, A.S., & Dowling, C.M. 2017. *Unhealthy politics: The battle over evidence-based medicine*. Princeton University Press: Princeton and Oxford.

Porter, M.E. & Kaplan, R.S. 2016. How to pay for health care. *Harvard Business Review*, July–August, 98(4): 88–100.

Potter, W. 2010. *Deadly spin*. Bloomsbury Press: New York.

Quadagno, J. 2008. Why the United States has no national health insurance: Stakeholder mobilization against the welfare state, 1945–1996. In C. Harrington & C.L. Estes (eds.), *Health policy: Crisis and reform in the*

U.S. health care delivery system, pp. 419–426, Fifth Edition. Jones and Bartlett Publishers: Sudbury, MA.

Rogers, W.A. 2007. Editorial: The tangled web of medical and commercial interests. *Health Expectations*, 10: 1–3.

Rosenthal, E. 2017. *An American sickness: How healthcare became a big business and how you can take it back*. Penguin Press: New York.

Saini, V., Garcia-Armesto, S., Klemperer, D., Paris, V., Elshaug, A.G., Brownlee, S., Ioannidis, J.P.A., & Fisher, E.S. 2017. Drivers of poor medical care. *Lancet*, 390: 178–190.

Shrank, W.H., Rogstad, T.L., & Parekh, N. 2019. Waste in the US health care system: Estimated costs and potential savings. *JAMA*, 322(15): 1501–1509.

Solman, P. 2017. Economics correspondent of PBS talks to Elisabeth Rosenthal, the author of "An American Sickness". Why the U.S. pays more for health care than the rest of the world. April 27.

Wagner, P.J., Jester, D.N., Albritton, T.A., Fincher, R.M., & Mosley, C.M. 2005. Emotional intelligence changes during medical school. *Teaching and Learning in Medicine*, 17(4): 391–395.

9 Medical Device Manufacturers

The device manufacturers have followed closely the pharmaceuticals' business model and took it a few steps further (Rosenthal, 2017). Common medical devices include artificial knees and hips, coronary stents, pacemakers, and the like. Like pharmaceuticals, they spend liberally on lobbying to buy favors from legislators. While many people might have heard of the Pharmaceuticals Research and Manufacturers of America (PhRMA) and its role, they are less likely to have heard of the Advanced Medical Technology Association (AdvaMed) or the Medical Device Manufacturers Association. These professional associations of device manufacturers have carved out a lucrative corner of medicine that has escaped any attempt to cost control and scrutiny. The device manufacturers have become the darlings of venture capital as there has been a proliferation of device patents.

Due to the lobbying efforts by device manufacturers, there is less scrutiny of new devices than of new drugs, even though the most drugs can be stopped in an instant in case of an adverse effect, which is not the case with medical devices as they are permanently implanted in the body (Rosenthal, 2017).

Given the way the US health care industry operates, the medical device manufacturers have found a fertile ground in the current health care system for their rapid growth, irrespective of whether the new devices are safe or not. Like pharmaceutical companies, device makers have developed sophisticated lobbying campaigns, often employing their own team of lobbyists in addition to hiring outside firms for specific issues. In 2019, the medical device industry employed 460 lobbyists and spent $40.2 million up from $26 million in 2017 (*Center of Responsive Politics*, 2020). The industry lobbying includes low taxes on devices, increased insurance coverage and reimbursement of devices, and exemptions from approval by the FDA for bringing new devices to the market.

DOI: 10.4324/9781003112204-11

The medical device sector has quietly matured, devising new financing models and methods that have escaped in-depth scrutiny. Medical devices essentially have no fixed price. These could rationally sell for a few hundred dollars, but sometimes cost more than a small house. The huge, notional number of the bill for any implant or procedure is the result of negotiations by a long list of intermediaries and their business decisions (Callahan, 2009).

In recent years, the growth in medical device spending has been above that for pharmaceuticals. And with the aging of the US accompanied by changes in obesity, these patterns are likely to get stronger. The medical device industry is highly concentrated that gives its members some monopoly power in setting the prices of their devices (Starr, 2017).

Other significant features of the medical device industry are outlined in the following sections.

A Tight-Knit Oligopoly

Device manufacturers are a tight-knit oligopoly with nearly absolute control of distribution. There are a dozen of large drug makers and hundreds of small ones, but only a handful of huge device manufacturers dominate the global market. Experts jokingly call them "the cartel" (Rosenthal, 2017). The major medical device manufactures in the US include Medtronic, DePuy Synthes, Fresenius, Philips Healthcare, GE Healthcare, Siemens Healthineers, Cardinal Health, and Stryker.

Nexus with Physicians

The marginal benefit for physicians to prescribe most drugs is small, unless the treatment is administered in a hospital setting, but the marginal benefit of prescribing a device is far larger. A treatment based on recommendation of a medical device involves surgery of some sort. Consequently, medical devices have been a boon to cardiologists and orthopedic surgeons who make millions of dollars from these treatments.

The medical device industry counts surgical specialty associations among its most important allies. It forms tight, codependent relationships with cardiologists and orthopedic surgeons (Rosenthal, 2017). Orthopedics is not a high science like neurology, but it is more like a precision carpentry. Thanks largely to device makers, orthopedic departments of hospitals have become their cash cows.

The device manufacturers encourage many physician group practices to form physician-owned distributorships, a new type of a company to cut out the layers of middlemen (Callahan, 2009). This way physicians buy implants through their distributorship and resell them to hospitals and surgery centers where they practice and install them in patients for twice as much.

Shoddy Oversight by FDA

Each year, flaws are found in thousands of medical devices. For example, the FDA posted more than 2,000 recalls of medical devices last year, warning about how to avoid possible injuries or even deaths. The US made medical devices are causing serious injuries and pain overseas (Siegel, Lehren, & Fitzpatrick, 2018). The US medical device makers sell their products overseas as 'export only' devices. While export only devices do not require the FDA approval, patients overseas assume so and as a result are more trusting of these devices only to find later that this is not the case.

The current system of evaluation and regulation of medical devices is flawed; it may be okay for toasters and kettles but is inadequate for treatments that affect patients' quality of life and can cause even death (Godlee, 2011). There is a lack of transparency over what tests are done before a device is approved. According to the FDA's own statement, "new devices are less likely than drugs to have their safety established clinically before they are marketed".

Unethical Behavior

Device makers, like pharmaceuticals, sometimes subtly manipulate patients and other times perpetuate myths that help device makers sell more of their products (Richtman, 2018; Rosenthal, 2017). Further, they lobby politicians to make sure that the voices of the people and their concerns about bad medicine (harmful procedures/products or costly procedures with minimal benefits) are suppressed (Callahan, 2009; Whitaker, 2018).

Conclusion

The device manufacturers have followed closely PhRMA's business model. As one would expect, the medical device manufacturers have found a fertile ground in the current health system for their rapid growth, irrespective of whether the new devices are safe and effective. They have built sophisticated lobbying arms, often employing their own team of lobbyists in addition to hiring outside firms for specific issues. The industry employed 460 lobbyists and spent $40.2 million in 2019. It lobbied for low taxes on devices, increased insurance coverage and reimbursement for the devices, and exemptions from approval by the FDA for bringing new devices to the market. The device manufacturers establish close relationships with physicians by encouraging physician group practices to form physician-owned distributorships that raise conflict of interest concerns.

References

Callahan, D. 2009. *Taming the beloved beast: How medical technology costs are destroying our health care system.* Princeton University Press: Princeton, NJ.

Center for Responsive Politics. 2018. Opensecrets.org.

Godlee, F. 2011. Editor's choice: The trouble with medical devices. *BMJ,* 342: d3123.

Richtman, M. 2018. Big pharma's cash flood is drowning seniors. *CNN.* April 3.

Rosenthal, E. 2017. *An American sickness: How healthcare became a big business and how you can take it back.* Penguin Press: New York.

Siegal, E.R., Lehren, A.W., & Fitzpatrick, S. 2018. How can a medical device deemed unsafe in another country still be sold in the U.S.? *NBC News.* November 27.

Starr, P. 2017. *The social transformation of American medicine: The rise of sovereign profession and the making of a vast industry* (2nd edition). Basic Books: New York.

Whitaker, B. 2018. EX-DEA agent: Opioid crisis fueled by drug industry and congress. *CBS News, 60 Minutes.* June 17.

10 American Public

The American public needs to be considered as one of the main players in the US health care system, because, ultimately, they are the ones who receive health care and who pay for it directly or indirectly. Significant issues related to the role of the American public in the current dysfunction in the US health care system, if any, include: (1) habits, attitudes, and lifestyle of Americans; (2) commonly harbored myths about the US health care system; (3) systematic shaping/manipulation of the attitudes of the American public by the system insiders; and (4) the prevalent biomedical model.

Habits, Attitudes, and Lifestyle of the Americans

On the face of it, the dysfunction in the US health care system may lie at least partly with the American values and attitudes, in other words, with the American society. The American health care is termed as radically American: individualistic, scientifically ambitious, market intoxicated, suspicious of government, and profit driven (Callahan, 2009). Any attempt to control the prices brings outcries of "socialized medicine" because of Americans' strong beliefs in free-market and unbridled entrepreneurism (Patashnik, Gerber, & Dowling, 2017).

The "cultural narcissism" or "unique feature of Americans' genetic makeup" has been suggested to be the reason for Americans' denial of the inevitability of death (Leifer, 2014), with the result that the US ends up spending dramatically high on health care near the end-of-life. As doctors wage an unwinnable battle, more and more resources are consumed. The patient undergoes more interventions but fares no better.

Just like other new technological gadgets, the Americans have been suggested to value the latest medical technologies (new medical

DOI: 10.4324/9781003112204-12

gadgets, latest drugs, devices, and five-star amenities in hospitals). The use of new health care technologies has contributed much to the ever-increasing cost of health care in the US in the last couple of decades, without any concomitant benefits. Instead, new medical technologies have been attributed to lead to poorer health care outcomes (Bradley & Taylor, 2013).

Lifestyle of Americans of eating junk food, a lot of it, and lack of exercise have been suggested other explanations for the higher costs of health care and poorer clinical outcomes. The US is a chronically ill nation with the sedentary lifestyle of Americans exacerbating the health care problems. Although not a panacea for all that ails individuals' health, exercise comes closer to a health-inducing tonic than any other intervention. But it seems that Americans do not get enough of it.

Then there is a suggestion of the entrenched culture of consuming more health care (see Chapter 3). Many Americans even insist on certain treatments or procedures despite there being no correct pathways (Patashnik et al., 2017).

It may seem from the above descriptions that the Americans might have gotten a system that they very much deserve. But upon closer scrutiny, the role of the American public in the dysfunction of the US health care system is somewhat complicated. Prevailing myths about the US health care system that have been perpetuated by system insiders, continuing efforts by system insiders to shape and manipulate attitudes of American public, and the prevalent biomedical model of care in the US may suggest that the problem may be more with the system insiders than with the American public as discussed in the following section.

The Commonly Harbored Myths about the US Health Care System

Several myths about the US health care system flourish because of the prevailing public attitude fueled by the powerful insiders of the system (Geyman, 2008). These myths are a major hurdle to debating and bringing about the necessary change in the system:

a   **The US has the best health care system in the world.** This view is not only untenable but also arrogant toward countries with better-performing health care systems. Since the current US health care system is malfunctioning, it requires a fundamental restructuring, which poses a threat to the stakeholders in the present system – hospitals, pharmaceuticals/device makers, physicians, and private health insurers. To protect their trough, the system insiders make nice claims such as the US health care system is the best in the world and attack reform proposals by raising concerns such as the changes in the system would lead to overly intrusive role of government, threat to the physician–patient relationship, and long waiting lines.

b   **Everyone gets care anyhow.** The truth is that a significant number of Americans get suboptimal care or no care at all. According to one estimate, 45,000 deaths occur annually due to lack of access as this has been suggested to be associated with greater risk of death in uninsured adults by 40 percent (Meissner, 2013).

c   **There is no rationing of health care in the US like other universal payer systems.** The current system denies services to those who cannot pay for them. Thus, the tacit rationing of health care is happening based on the income level of Americans.

d   **The current US health care system is a free-market system.** The current US health care system is not a free-market system by any stretch of imagination. It is a hodgepodge of capitalism and socialism, in which greed of capitalism and inefficiency of socialism fuse together (see Chapter 2). The industry keeps suggesting as if the current health care system is a free-market system and any proposal to reform it would result in 'socialized medicine'. Leifer (2014; p. 157) notes:

> We have been propagandized to believe that health care is market-driven industry, as such, will course correct to meet the demands of the marketplace. As part of our collective brainwashing, we've also been led to believe that any significant changes to the current system may move us closer to socialized medicine, which has been highly demonized.

e   **The free market can resolve the problems in the US health care system.** Touted as the 'American way', there is a belief that a private, competitive market exists in health care. Yet there is inconvertible evidence that the US health care markets are not functioning well (Geyman, 2008). It is hard to think of a more unfair financial arrangement between the patients and the health care system, one in which the buyer side is virtually defenseless vis-à-vis the supply side, and it is hard to imagine that any other country would allow it (Reinhardt, 2019). Current health care markets in the US yield distributional advantages for health care providers, suppliers, insurers, and more affluent and healthier Americans. The natural alliance between providers, suppliers, and higher-income citizens in support of the private financing of health care leaves the burden of financing care for the sick and uninsured to the public sector. The farther the system continues its current trajectory, the more difficult it is to finance the basic health care services for sick and lower-income people through a smaller risk pool.

f **The US health care system is basically healthy, so incremental change will address its problems.** Incrementalism has been the prevailing approach to health care reform for at least 50 years in the US, and it is still the most politically popular. Advocated by the powerful system insiders, incremental changes are put in place, which fail to address the fundamental problems of the system.

The role of American public cannot be fully and appropriately understood without talking about the health care industry spin machine.

Shaping/Manipulating of Views/Attitudes of American Public by the Industry Spin Machine

I too held the view that Americans have gotten a health care system that they fully deserve. Upon delving deeper into the US health care system, I feel somewhat different. The health care industry has shaped/manipulated the attitudes of Americans via its spin machine and misinformation campaigns. By perpetuating attitudes favorable to the industry, it has been greatly successful in diminishing threats of a health care reform that could quash hundreds of billions of dollars in profit that the industry makes each year.

The health care industry's misinformation and fearmongering campaigns began in earnest with the Truman's administration in 1945 and continue till today. Private health insurers have pursued promotional efforts to perpetuate myths that amount to conspiracy theories (see *deadly spin* in Chapter 6). They persistently promote that the US health care system is the best in the world with the implication that it does not need to be changed. Thanks to their relentless efforts, they have succeeded in making Americans believe that their system is the best in the world, despite the US having the lowest levels of satisfaction with health care as compared to other industrialized countries (Reinhardt, 2019).

The rhetoric of 'socialized medicine' is ramped up anytime there is talk of reforming the health system. Private health insurers went after the Affordable Care Act (Obamacare) by funding the efforts of the Tea Party, which passed the bills to repeal the American Affordable Act in the US House about 60 times. It might not be an exaggeration that the Tea Party movement was to a significant extent the creation of the private health insurance industry.

The industry pays consultants and pollsters millions of dollars to craft and test phrases in focus groups and surveys that could be used in spreading misinformation. For example, the industry has found that the phrases 'the best health care system in the world' and 'a government takeover of the health care system' resonate with public. Thus, the industry uses them often in their misinformation campaigns to sway public opinion (see Chapter 6). Biden's observation in his Presidential Inaugural Speech on January 20, 2021 aptly describes the above behavior: There is truth and there are lies, lies told for power and for profit.

Potter (2010) offers a classic example of the spin machine. In the heat of the debate on the 2009 Affordable Care Act, at one event sponsored by the insurance industry, several angry protestors carried signs demanding that the government keep its hands 'off my Medicare', without realizing that they were enrolled in the country's biggest government-run health care program. Potter (2009) cautions that, whenever you hear a politician or pundit use the term "government-run health care" and warn that the creation of a public health insurance option would "lead us down the path to socialism", know that the original source of the sound bite most likely is some public relations department of a private health insurer.

The Prevalent Biomedical Model of Health Care in the US

The prevalent biomedical model of health focuses mostly on biological factors and excludes psychological, environmental, and social influences. This model does not consider individual's lifestyle or their environment, both of which play a major role in the physical and mental wellness of individuals.

The single-minded focus in the biomedical model is on treating patients after they get sick. Prevention as a source of good health of individuals does not receive adequate attention. There are clear consequences of doing so. America is a chronically ill nation and ranks high in poor lifestyle choices by its citizens that eventually catch up and take a major toll on their health and well-being. The system, however, makes more money when more people are sick rather than healthy; preventive care does not seem rewarding financially and thus is neither practiced nor encouraged.

Other developed nations spend about twice as much on public health as they spend on medical care, which is the opposite of what the US does; it spends about twice as much on medical care than public health. The implication is that other countries spend more efforts on preventive care. Yes, the US citizens can be blamed for their poor lifestyle choices and habits. However, if the system does not provide the right information and educate people, larger public will remain ignorant and keep pursuing the bad lifestyle choices. People can be educated not only about the lifestyle but also about various illnesses and early detection. Doing so would make population healthier and reduce the demand for health care.

Americans believe that doctors are experts who are empathetic and concerned about helping people, and do not see economic incentives as a primary factor of doctors' behavior (Patashnik, Gerber, & Dowling, 2017). Because most Americans believe 'doctor knows best', they tend to have confidence in the advice of doctors, not only about individual medical problems, but also about broader health care reform issues. A health care encounter involves a physician and a patient. The more complicated the disease or diagnosis, the greater the information or knowledge gap between the physician and the patient. Asymmetry of information combined with vulnerability arising from the patient being sick consigns a patient at the mercy of the physician/medical profession. In such a case, the only saving grace for the patient may be the ethical behavior on the part of physician. If, for any reason, ethical behavior on the part of the physician is compromised, the patient is not likely to get the optimal care. That is why ethical behavior is stressed and expected so much from physicians. However, the ethical behavior on the part of physicians is not given in view of what the current US health care system has morphed into with an overemphasis on profit. That is why, overtreatments are one major category of waste in the US health care system.

Conclusion

Habits, attitudes, and lifestyles of the Americans are said to contribute the US health care system dysfunction. It is said that the American health care is radically American – it is individualistic, suspicious of government, and profit driven. A single-payer system is said not to fit American values. This chapter notes that, while some of these explanations may be plausible, upon closer scrutiny, they are not a satisfactory explanation of the dysfunction in the US health care system. The fault for the health care dysfunction very much lies with the system insiders – physicians and the biomedical model, private health insurers, pharmaceutical companies, and hospitals and hospital networks. The system insiders feed misinformation and propagate and perpetuate myths to keep the status quo. To thwart any reform of the system, key players keep telling American public that Americans have the best health care system, despite it being one of the laggards. The prevalent biomedical model single-mindedly focuses on treating patients after they get sick. Because of the lack of proper information, most Americans do not understand well how to take care of their body and stay healthy. They do not understand what kind of reforms would improve the system, thus making any worthwhile reform of the US health care system difficult.

References

Bradley, E.H. & Taylor, L.A. 2013. *The American health care paradox: Why spending more is getting us less.* Public Affairs: New York.

Callahan, D. 2009. *Taming the beloved beast: How medical technology costs are destroying our health care system.* Princeton University Press: Princeton, NJ.

Geyman, J.P. 2008. Myths as barriers to health care reform in the United States. In C. Harrington & C.L. Estes (eds.), *Health policy: Crisis and reform in the U.S. health care delivery system,* pp. 407–413, Fifth Edition. Jones and Bartlett Publishers: Sudbury, MA.

Leifer, J. 2014. *The myth of modern medicine: The alarming truth about American health Care.* Rowman & Littlefield: Lanham, MD.

Meissner, J. 2013. Unraveling the crisis in American healthcare. *Vital News* (Seattle), Spring.

Patashnik, E.M., Gerber, A.S., & Dowling, C.M. 2017. *Unhealthy politics: The battle over evidence-based medicine.* Princeton University Press: Princeton and Oxford.

Potter, W. 2009. The health care industry vs health reform. http://wendellpotter.com/2009/06/the-health-care-industry-vs-health-reform/

Potter, W. 2010. *Deadly spin.* Bloomsbury Press: New York.

Reinhardt, U.E. 2019. *Priced out: The economic and ethical costs of American health care.* Princeton University Press: Princeton, NJ.

Part 3

How to Fix the US Health Care System Dysfunction

This part of the book consists of three chapters with each chapter offering suggestions to reform the US health care system dysfunction – addressing crony capitalism, root cause of the problem; health insurance, payment, and pricing arrangements; and well-informed American citizenry.

DOI: 10.4324/9781003112204-13

11 Addressing Crony Capitalism, Root Cause of the Dysfunction

Capitalism, like any powerful tool, could be greatly used or abused. For harnessing capitalism, a fair, transparent, well-formulated institutional framework is the key. In other words, to unleash the power of free markets requires adult supervision (Henderson, 2020). Apparently, capitalism has gone rogue in the US health care system. In 2019, the US health care industry employed the largest number of lobbyists (2,826) and spent the most amount on lobbying ($604 million) among all 13 industrial sectors in the US economy. Olson (1982) argued that "pure" capitalism, if it even exists, becomes politically "sclerotic" by the slow accretion of protection arrangements organized by narrow, specific groups. The resulting crony capitalism is in the mutual interest of large interest groups and units of the government/politicians who collude with these interest groups (Munger & Villarreal-Diaz, 2019). The way the US political and economic systems have evolved, lobbying now offers one of the highest rates of return on investment (English, 2013; Salter, 2014). No wonder, lobbying, grifting, and crony capitalism have come to flourish in the US political and economic spheres.

Crony capitalism has become ubiquitous in the US economy and powerful business and interest groups have captured the American democracy and political institutions (English, 2013; Mitchell, 2012; Salter, 2014). Political parties and candidates need to raise tons of money to be competitive and win elections. The reality they face is that they have got to begin raising money for the next term the day after they have been elected for the current term. The packing order, chairing or being a member of an influential Congressional committee, depends on who brings in more money from business and interest groups.

Money is the oxygen of politics. Nearly $24 billion were spent by federal candidates, political action committees, and party committees in the 2020 US election (Enten, 2021). In 2016, the amount spent was $9 billion. Presidential candidates alone raised $4 billion in 2020 as

DOI: 10.4324/9781003112204-14

compared to $2 billion in 2008. Since Supreme Court's Citizens United decision in 2010, the money in politics has been pouring at a mind-boggling scale. It seems that no amount of money is enough to contest an election. In 2020, Joe Biden's and Donald Trump's Presidential campaign committees raised $1 billion and $774 million, respectively. The North Carolina senate race in 2020 saw a spending of $265 million by the two candidates and outside groups. The Iowa senate race involved a total spending of $218 million. The House races are no pushovers. In 2018, $42 million was spent in California's 39th District race and, in 2020, about $37 million was spent in New Mexico's 2nd District.

Where does this pile of money in the US elections come from and why? Politicians from both major political parties are heavily dependent on the money that they receive from the business and interest groups. In exchange, these business and interest groups want their pound of flesh. Chapter 2 suggests that crony capitalism (the government-granted favors) is a destructive force. It misdirects resources, impedes genuine economic progress, and breeds corruption. Business and interest groups do not seek the same policies as average citizens, rather their positions on issues are aligned against the citizens. Business and interest groups that donate a lot of money to political campaigns are found to seek rent and be less attentive to consumer needs. Their products, services, and ideas may not be good to compete in the free market (Mitchell, 2012). Thus, to ply their business, these business and interest groups spend efforts and resources to rig the policy and rules in their favor.

The failure of American political institutions, because of the undue influence of interest groups, lies at the heart of the US health care system dysfunction (Harrington & Estes, 2008). Chapter 4 reasons that powerful interest groups – private health insurers, pharmaceuticals/medical device manufacturers, hospitals/nursing homes, and physicians/medical professionals – have fully captured the US health policy. Because they set the rules of the game (e.g., prices of health care treatments, procedures, and services) for themselves, they make hundreds of billion dollars every year. The US health care industry spends the most money on political donations and lobbying among all US industrial sectors and by far. Over the years, it has become the piggy bank of political parties and candidates belonging to the two parties. Thus, if Americans want the Congress to act on a reform agenda, they need to focus on reforming political institutions and minimizing the influence of special interest groups to make it easier for a democratic majority to get ground-breaking legislations enacted (Harrington & Estes, 2008). In addition, fixing the US health care system would require educating and informing the American citizenry and good, determined individuals to force both US political and health care systems to recalibrate (Piketty, 2020).

> There is no greater threat to American economic competitiveness and social progress – no greater threat to the combination of free-market economies and liberal democracies that has delivered more human advancements than any other system – than Americans' passive acceptance of a failed political system.
>
> (Gehl & Porter, 2020)

Given the failure of American political system and undue influence of powerful interest groups in the US health care industry, it takes a lot of courage even to muse reforming it. Having said so, a lot of Americans seem tired of the current US political and health care systems. An extremely high level of desperation in the society is needed to move it to act and reform these two systems. American society may already be there or would be there soon, and there are opportunities for well-meaning individuals, groups, and businesses to get into the act of transforming the US health care system, which is long overdue.

There are three possible ways to bring about necessary change in the political system: (1) the role of business, (2) political campaign reform, and (3) politics by principle and influx of entrepreneurs.

The Role of Business

Since business and interest groups play an important role in perpetuating and unleashing crony capitalism, the solution to this problem may lie with them. Gehl and Porter (2020) express optimism that the situation is approaching a turning point and businesses increasingly share voters' frustration with the two-party political system as it has failed time and again to deliver sound policy. The predominant business model of maximizing profit and shareholder value too has been found lacking and is giving way to a model in which businesses are supposed to be socially responsible. Gehl and Porter conducted a survey in 2019 to assess the attitudes of business leaders using a sample of about 5,000 alumni of the Harvard Business School. The survey findings revealed that more than half of the respondents thought the business was degrading the political system by reinforcing partisanship and favoring corporate special interests, and 69 percent believed business's engagement in politics undermined public trust in business.

To reform the system, most of the leaders agreed that: (1) companies should engage with politics to improve the overall business environment and level-playing field that advance the public interest rather than their own narrow business interest; (2) the trade associations should focus more on improving the business environment and less on advancing the interest of member companies; (3) the business community should spend less on lobbying; (4) companies should reconsider corporate spending levels on elections and should channel support to problem-solving candidates, not partisans; and (5) companies should not encourage employees to vote for or contribute directly to companies' preferred candidates in elections. These above measures seem practical and can help improve the political system significantly. Thus, well-meaning businesses need to step up and support and advocate these measures and citizens must demand businesses to support issues and candidates that benefit the society rather than narrow interests.

Political Campaign Reforms, Repeal of Citizens United, and Small Donor Revolution

In 2010, the US Supreme Court in its Citizens United decision unleashed a wave of unlimited election spending that undermines American democracy by allowing outsized influence of corporate and wealthy individuals over ordinary Americans. The decision unless repealed would be destructive to democracy and spawn much greater crony capitalism in the US economy. The Supreme Court presumed that the spending, even when done by corporations, would not give rise to corruption or the appearance of corruption. It further presumed that the transparency could protect the public and would provide the means to hold candidates and their supporters accountable. The presumptions of the Supreme Court have turned out to be unfounded.

In the decade after the Citizens United decision, spending by outside individuals and groups have exploded and increased 14-fold (McPhail, 2020) and large amount of "dark money" from anonymous donors has distorted elections in favor of wealthy individuals against ordinary citizens (Massoglia, 2020). The Citizens United ruling unintendedly has fueled legalized corruption and loosened rules to allow even hostile foreign powers to launder money to support US political campaigns (Grayson, 2021). America's democratic institutions continue to face new threats from money increasingly flowing into US elections as well as efforts to erode what little transparency rules remain in place. Jon Tester, a US Senator from Montana who is an advocate for repealing United Citizens' decision, notes: "For too long, dark money has played an outsized role in our politics – and with disastrous results ... We need real hardworking families, not billionaires and corporations, deciding our elections ... our elections are not for sale" (2021).

The small donor revolution is one solution to the problem. Obama raised more than $1 billion online from small donors for his two presidential campaigns. Bernie Sanders and Donald Trump were successful in 2016, and various candidates in the 2020 election raised a lot of money from small donors that could be thought of representing the interests of common citizens. Small donor campaign contributions in the 2020 election showed a substantial jump from previous elections, accounting for 22.5 percent of all donations. This is a healthy trend and shows that citizens are taking more interest and fighting for issues that matter to them.

Politics by Principle and Influx of Entrepreneurs

Munger and Villarreal-Diaz (2019) observe that the road to cronyism leads directly through capitalism and make a clear distinction between 'crony' capitalism and 'real' capitalism. According to these scholars, there are a couple of plausible solutions to crony capitalism. One, to inculcate entrepreneurial ethos not to want to become rent seekers and to constrain state actors not to sell off rents in the first place, which means 'politics by principle, not interest'. The celebrated US business model promotes seeking self-interest with guile and glorifies greed. The result has been an erosion of ethics in business and society.

The second solution that Munger and Villarreal-Diaz advocate is that the strength of capitalism in a democratic society is the constant influx of creative individuals who demand adequate conditions to advance their productive efforts. An example is the recent nonprofit joint venture 'Haven' founded by Amazon, Berkshire Hathaway, and J.P. Morgan Chase, which is aimed at improving health care for their 1.2 million combined employees (Farr, 2019). The goal of the joint venture is to leverage technology to provide simplified, high-quality, and transparent health care at a reasonable cost. The new company aims to be free from profit-making incentives and constraints that undermine quality of patient care. The three companies have the potential to disrupt the health care industry status quo (Popken & Bayly, 2018) as they have the capital, technology, and managerial expertise to bring efficiencies and improvements to health care delivery to serve their employees and offer an example for others to follow.

Conclusion

The US health care system is a microcosm of the American society. Many things that afflict American society also afflict the US health care system and vice versa. The US political system has become polarized and corrupt, preventing any meaningful reform at both federal and state levels. The situation is made worse by the amount of money interest groups plow into the system to capture health policy. Crony capitalism needs to be the part of the discussion and a remedy to truly fixing the health care system lies therein. Businesses and interest groups are coming to the realization that political system is not working and they might be contributing to its dysfunction. Thus, they need to take responsibility to reform it. The Supreme Court's Citizens United decision has unleashed dark money into US politics and made the political system much worse. It must be repealed. Its destructive influence could be neutralized to some extent by the small donor revolution. Politics by principle rather than interest is one plausible solution in which entrepreneurs are empowered not to want to become rent seekers and state actors are constrained from selling rents. The other solution is the constant influx of creative individuals in a democratic capitalistic society who demand adequate conditions to advance their productive efforts.

References

English, W. 2013. *Institutional corruption and the crisis of liberal democracy*. Working Paper No. 15. Edmond J. Safra Center for Ethics. Harvard University: Boston, MA.

Enten, H. 2021. How Trump made people care about politics again. *CNN.* January 2.

Farr, C. 2019. Everything we know about Haven, the Amazon joint venture to revamp health care. *CNBC.* March 14.

Gehl, K.M. & Porter, M.E. 2020. Fixing U.S. politics: What businesses can – and must – do to revitalize democracy. *Harvard Business Review*, July–August, 115–125.

Grayson, D. 2021. Tweet. The Citizens United ruling LEGALIZED #corruption, loosening rules to allow hostile foreign powers to launder $$ to support US political campaigns. Face with symbols over mouth. February 11.

Harrington, C. & Estes, C.L. 2008. *Health policy: Crisis and reform in the U.S. health care delivery system*. Fifth Edition. Jones and Bartlett Publishers: Sudbury, MA.

Henderson, R. 2020. *Reimagining capitalism in a world on fire*. Public Affairs: New York.

Massoglia, A. 2020. 'Dark money' in politics skyrocketed in the wake of Citizens United. Center for Responsive Politics. January 27. www.opensecrets.org/news/2020/01/dark-money-10years-citizens-united/

McPhail, S. 2020. Citizens United allowed money in politics to explode. It's up to us to stop it. *Citizensforethics.org.* January 21.

Mitchell, M. 2012. *The pathology of privilege: The economic consequences of government favoritism.* A working Paper. Mercus Center, George Mason University: Arlington, VA.

Munger, M.C. & Villarreal-Diaz, M. 2019. The road to crony capitalism. *The Independent Review*, 23(3): 331–344.

Olson, M. 1982. *The rise and decline of nations: Economic growth, stagflation, and social rigidities.* Yale University Press: New Haven, CT.

Piketty, T. 2020. *Capital and ideology.* Harvard University Press: Cambridge, MA.

Popken, B. & Bayly, L. 2018. Amazon, Chase, and Berkshire Hathaway partner to disrupt health care. *NBC.news.com.* January 30.

Salter, M.S. 2014. *Crony capitalism, American style: What are we talking about here?* Working Paper 15-025. Edmund J. Safra Center for Ethics, Harvard University: Boston, MA.

Tester, J. 2021. On 11th anniversary of Citizens United decision, Tester reaffirms commitment to cleaning up dark money politics. January 21.

12 Health Insurance, Payment, and Pricing Arrangements

Although health care systems all over the globe are poorly organized and perform worse than other industries, a comparison of national health care systems shows that some systems perform better than others. Especially, there is a cluster of developed countries that have achieved better outcomes at lower cost than the US (see Chapter 1). These countries include Australia, France, Germany, the Netherlands, New Zealand, Norway, Sweden, and the United Kingdom. The per capita cost and the health care expenditure as the share of gross domestic product in these countries are about the same but about one-half of that in the US. It would seem that these countries have found a better solution to the health care problem than the US. By the way, these countries are democracies, hold individualistic values, and all rely on capitalism as the underlying economic model. Americans are living the fantasy thinking that America's free-market system could provide actual health care for its people through a for-profit structure (Dubois, 2010). They may be better off looking at the health care arrangements of other countries who are managing their health care systems better than the US.

Chapter 1 noted that the current US health care system is exorbitantly expensive, a source of anxiety, insecurity, and despair for many Americans; is wasteful and starving other sectors of the economy; does not provide any better and safer clinical outcomes than other systems; and has scam-like properties. Further, Chapter 2 pointed out that the US health care system is a peculiar mix of capitalism and socialism, borrowing the worst elements of greed and inefficiency, respectively, from capitalism and socialism. Big interest groups – hospitals/nursing homes, pharmaceuticals/device makers, physicians/medical professionals, and private health insurers – have rigged the system in such a way that risks and costs of doing business are borne by the US taxpayers, but profits are pocketed by the interest groups. Given that the

DOI: 10.4324/9781003112204-15

spending by federal and state governments in the US health care system constitutes about 50 percent of the total spending, the current system is not a free-market system by any stretch of imagination. Thus, fearing reforms in the system as 'government takeover of health care' or the US becoming a 'communist' or 'socialist' country are quite ridiculous. If anything, Americans must fear if the current system has become a socialism for the large corporate interests.

Chapter 2 considered the enormous waste in the US health care system, which is approaching a trillion dollar annually, and identified its four major drivers: administrative complexity ($266 billion); pricing failures of health care procedures, treatments, drugs, and services ($236 billion); overtreatments ($89 billion); and failures of care delivery and coordination ($130 billion to $244 billion) (Shrank, Rogstad, & Parekh, 2019). Thus, if we are serious about reforming the system, we must address these drivers of annual waste/dysfunction in the US health care system. We must understand though that there is a tremendous pressure from powerful players to maintain the status quo since eliminating a dollar of waste in the health care system usually means reducing someone's income (Patashnik, Gerber, & Dowling, 2017).

> So health care reform of any kind will always be met with a lot of resistance from inside the system. All of that money isn't just wasted – it's going into the pockets of a lot of people who will fight very hard to keep things as they are.
>
> (Belk, 2018)

Further, it is not that the powerful insiders are not aware of the waste that they cause in the system. They do but they nonetheless pursue health policies and legislation that, although lead to waste in the system, earn them billions of dollars. Chapters 4–9 delved into how the main players in the system have contributed to the US health care dysfunction. The rest of this chapter proposes solutions to overcome the dysfunction in the US health care caused by various system insiders. Let us look at the major drivers of waste/dysfunction in the US health care system and how to fix the waste/dysfunction arising from them.

Administrative Complexity

Private insurance plans contribute to the most of health care waste resulting from the administrative complexity to the tune of $266 billion (see Chapter 6). Thus, any attempt to reform the system must look at the health insurance arrangements and would require overhauling them.

Chapter 6 laid out the history as to how private health insurers, in alliance with other system insiders (e.g., physicians and health care providers) have been against reforming the US health care system. They unleash the spin machine whenever there is any talk of transforming the US health care system. The reason is simple. Private health insurers have unfettered corporate power as they control much of the money that goes into system and make hundreds of billions of dollars every year. The US health care system is an "administrative monstrosity, a truly bizarre mélange of thousands of payers with [different] payments systems" (Aaron, cited in Reinhardt, 2019). Because of the variety and complexity of private health insurance plans, health care providers need to employ hundreds or even a thousand or more of billing and coding clerks.

Private health insurance companies in other countries are heavily regulated requiring them to offer uniform fees to customers to prevent them from engaging in more pernicious forms of practices (Quadagno, 2008). This is not the case in the US, where private insurance companies use sophisticated forms of medical 'underwriting' to set premiums and skim off more desirable employee groups and individuals. The US is the only nation that fails to guarantee coverage of medical services, rations extensively by ability to pay, and allows the private insurance industry to serve as a gatekeeper to the health care system. It should come as no surprise that private health insurers are milking the system in the name of health care and at the expense of American public.

Most nations have much simpler health insurance and payment arrangements. Usually, there is a heavily government-regulated social insurance scheme covering 90-95 percent of the population, with uniform fee schedule and rules, and small private insurance market outside the social insurance scheme used by mostly upper-income households. For example, Canadian citizens get an insurance card that they can use anywhere in Canada. Further, they have not to worry if they lose or change job or move. They get another card issued promptly. In fact, there is a good example for private health insurers from within the US health care system itself. The Medicare is so simple to administer and its administrative costs are one-third of the private health insurance plans. Countries, like Israel and the Netherlands, which rely wholly on private health insurers as gatekeepers of health care to their citizens, closely regulate private health insurers. Both countries set, enforce, and mediate uniform fees and fair policies and guidelines to manage competition among private health insurers. By having clear rules and level-playing field, both Israel and the Netherlands have succeeded in bringing market forces in their health care systems into play.

Private health insurers have 'captured' legislators at both federal and state levels. They, in collusion with politicians and health care providers, are taking American citizens for a ride. Private health insurers would have to be forced to give up their hegemony. The uniform fee schedules and rules that make the system simple are an imperative. A coalition of physicians and American citizens seems a possible way to counter the power and influence of private health insurers. Fed up, frustrated, and awakened physicians and citizens need to take the fight to private health insurers to ensure fair and uniform fee schedules, rules, and policies. A well thought-out public option along with a proper framework for the roles of private insurers may be necessary to generate a competitive dynamic which is lacking in the US health care system at present.

Pricing failure of health care procedures, drugs, and services amounting to about $235 billion in waste annually is another major driver of the waste/dysfunction in the US health care system (Shrank, Rogstad, & Parekh, 2019).

Pricing Failures of Health Care Procedures, Treatments, Drugs, and Services

In the US, prices of most procedures, treatments, drugs, and services are at least twice or more than those of identical procedures or services in other developed countries. This is so because of the absence of transparency and competitive markets in the US. Three major sources of price failures include highly overpriced drugs, overbilling or surprise billing, and more expensive treatments and procedures instead of equally effective cheaper treatments and procedures. The medication pricing failure contributes to the bulk of the waste to the tune of $170 billion. Drug companies are the ones that benefit most from the medication pricing failure, but health care providers and physicians also benefit to a significant extent. For example, a tablet of Tylenol at an academic medical center could be billed as much as $25. Health care providers benefit from medication pricing failures by prescribing a new and more expensive drug for a treatment, where a cheaper and equally effective generic drug is available. Payer-based health services and prices of laboratory tests and ambulatory services are other components of pricing failures taken together accounting for about $65 billion. These mainly pad up the revenues of health care providers and physicians.

Chapter 5 discussed in-depth that drug companies control politicians and legislators by contributing handsomely to the political campaigns. They have built mutually beneficial relationships with physicians, and they own the Food and Drug Administration (FDA). All this gives pharmaceutical firms unlimited power to fix the prices of their drugs and obstruct federal and state governments to negotiate meaningful prices for various medications. Thus, the political campaign reform is essential as discussed in Chapter 11 and FDA must be made to begin to behave like other federal agencies rather than being subservient to drug and medical device manufacturers. The current governance structure of FDA might require rethinking.

Chapter 7 laid out how poorly organized hospitals and other health care providers are and how deliberately opaque they are about the prices of procedures and services. They are adept at surprise billing and use the hospital charge master as an exploitative pricing tool. The US hospital market is superconcentrated meaning that hospitals can charge exorbitant prices for their services without losing customers. They have converted emergency room services, lab tests, and other ancillary services such as physical therapy into cash cows. Any further consolidation of health care providers must be immediately halted and ways how to foster fair and competitive hospital market, the hallmark of American ingenuity, must be looked at. The health care markets that are dominated by one major hospital or system must be opened to other health care providers.

The prices of medical procedures and treatments are set by the Specialty Society Relative Value Scale Update Committee of the for-profit American Medical Association (see Chapter 8). The US is the only country that has given the entire authority to set prices for health care treatments and services to a for-profit medical association. Every other country uses more appropriate price determination mechanisms involving committees representing the government, neutral experts, and the society. It should come as no surprise that most procedures, treatments, and services are far more expensive in the US than other countries. Obviously, the current system of setting prices of medical procedures and treatments by a for-profit association of physicians is farcical. Like other countries, a more representative body is needed and government bodies should be able to negotiate prices with various medical associations.

Drug companies, hospitals, and physicians in the US are given a free hand to the extent that they can even defraud customers if they want. Every other country has mechanisms to regulate the prices of drugs and hospital and physician services but not in the US. Of course, the prices of medical treatments and services in the US know only one way, going up. The decade after decade health care expenditures in the US have far outpaced the increase in the general rate of inflation. As discussed in Chapter 1, the increase in prices of medical services in last many decades has taken away any increase in real income of Americans. Obviously, pricing failures in the US health care system have occurred because there are no rules to curb them, the rules that every other country has implemented. The US must do the same.

Failures of Care Delivery and Coordination

The failures of care delivery and coordination contribute to annual waste in the system ranging from $130 billion to $244 billion (Shrank, Rogstad, & Parekh, 2019). This category of waste results chiefly from health care providers being poorly organized and managed and includes things like hospital acquired conditions and adverse events, clinician-related inefficiencies, lack of adoption of preventive care practices, unnecessary admissions and avoidable complications, and readmissions. Chapter 7 suggested that the US health care providers lack a culture of innovation. Their business model is tilted toward making money by rigging the system through favorable health legislation rather than making money by being efficient and producing affordable, high-quality products and services. In the last couple of decades, health care providers have focused on mergers and acquisitions, resulting in superconcentrated hospital market in the US. Hospitals in such a concentrated market can operate inefficiently and provide poor quality of care and still thrive. It should come as no surprise that US hospitals are behind other industries in their management practices by at least a decade or more (Khatri, Pasupathy, & Hicks, 2012).

Why do hospitals not care about more efficiencies and better management practices? The current system of payment, fee-for-service, rewards inefficient health care providers. Chapter 7 discussed the cost conundrum in US hospitals by contrasting two different models of care, namely, McAllen, Texas, and Mayo, Minnesota (Gawande, 2009). McAllen is a typical US hospital with emphasis on maximizing reimbursements rather than focusing on delivering safe and quality care by improving organization and management of their health care delivery system. Since efficiency is not emphasized, health care delivery is neither optimized nor well-coordinated, resulting in more expensive care. In contrast, Mayo is known for its exemplary model of care. It provides seamless, high-quality care efficiently. Because it is organized better, it incurs lower costs. It pays physicians a fixed salary so that they are not incentivized to prescribe more procedures and services to enhance hospital revenue. In 2006, McAllen got reimbursed about $15,000 per Medicare enrollee and Mayo got reimbursed only about $6,688 per Medicare enrollee. What a crazy system would allow such an outcome where a hospital providing much worse care get reimbursed more than twice as much as the other hospital that provides much better care?

Clearly, the current payment arrangement is nonsensical and must be changed. Other countries have used a couple of strategies effectively to rein in the abuses of the fee-for-service model. One mechanism is to stipulate an overall annual budget for health care providers. Canada and Germany use this strategy of global budgets for hospitals to curb runaway costs. Another way to restrain overtreatments resulting from the fee-for-service model is to have fixed salaries for physicians. In other countries, the proportion of the salary-based physicians is substantial unlike the US where most physicians practice based on fee-for-service basis. Further, Germany uses another cost containment measure in which it tracks and monitors data on physicians and penalizes those who resort to overtreatments.

Overtreatments or Overuse of Medicine

The waste resulting from the overuse of medicine ranges from $76 to $101 billion (Shrank, Rogstad, & Parekh, 2019). Chapters 7 and 8 argued that health care providers and physicians are the major culprits for overuse of medicine in the US health care system. In the absence of any specific controls or budget ceilings, both health care providers and physicians make more money by prescribing and providing more treatments, procedures, drugs, and services. Other countries have implemented mechanisms to curb overuse of medicine via instituting annual ceiling on hospital budgets and monitoring physicians' prescription patterns and penalizing physicians who overtreat patients. The large physician workforce in other countries earn their income from fixed salaries rather than from fee-for-service.

The above discussion of four key drivers of waste makes it clear that the powerful system insiders are gaming the system to their advantage. Thus, the greed has to be a huge part of the discussion and the remedy to truly fixing the entire health care system. Any effort short of that will be akin to taking an aspirin for cancer – not going to fix the real problem (Shaffer, 2017).

In addition to looking at the key drivers of waste/dysfunction in the system, there are some basic, practical solutions available to improve the US health care system.

Basic, Practical Solutions

Americans look for health care solutions in wrong places (Pearl, 2017). For example, hundreds of thousands of lives could be saved each year if doctors reduced common medical errors and maximized preventive medicine.

The American system of financing health care has far strayed from the original concept of insurance, which was to spread risk over a large pool of policyholders so that everyone, regardless of age or health, paid the same amount for coverage (Potter, 2010). Thus, following the basic principles of insurance could improve the US health care system significantly. Doing so would require meaningful restraints and regulations on private health insurers like in other countries, which obviously would be greatly resisted by the insurers.

The dysfunction in the US health care system is not that because the US lacks clinical knowledge and expertise. The US is way ahead in medical research and knowledge. The dysfunction is about how to organize the system more effectively. Thus, the solution to the dysfunction lies more in fixing organizational and management issues than medical/clinical issues. The US health care needs more expertise in management practices that continue to be ignored because of the hegemony of the clinical mindset. Health care organizations lag behind other industries in their organizational and management practices by a decade or more. As Gawande rightly notes: "Research on our health care system can save more lives in the next decade than bench science, research on the genome, stem-cell research, cancer vaccine research, and everything else we hear about on the news" (cited in Ronis, 2007). Unfortunately, most programs and initiatives to improve the system remain clinically driven such as precision medicine, which would consume a lot of resources, but might not improve the health care delivery to any significant extent.

The current system suffers from the problem of "other people's money" (Herzlinger, 2018). Often a patient ordering and receiving medical care mistakenly believes he or she is not the one paying for it. Free access to health care with no out-of-pocket requirements diminishes personal responsibilities, leaving no demand-side constraints. Price-conscious behavior, with the use of deductibles and co-pays, can be encouraged with little impact on health. France is using this strategy to contain health care costs. The co-pays in France are kept as high as 20–30 percent. People with low income who cannot afford high co-pays receive subsidies.

An analysis of health care systems across the globe suggests that the US would benefit by addressing the following critical elements: (a) a health safety net for all residents; (b) mechanisms that promote cost containment; and (c) ease in administration (Folland, Goodman, & Stano, 2013).

Conclusion

Obviously, health care markets in the US are functioning poorly. The present system is a refined form of a jungle raj rather than a properly regulated, functioning free market. It is not unlike many poorly governed systems that we see across the globe. The US health care system needs adult supervision, a lot of it. Otherwise, the system insiders would continue to plunder the American economy and citizens, the kind of things that we see in news in underdeveloped nations and economies. The misguided belief in Americans that all markets are always and everywhere necessarily efficient is patently false (Komlos, 2017). Clinging to an outdated ideology is harmful as evidenced by the unsatisfactory performance of the US health care system over many decades. The sources of waste and dysfunction in the US health care system are well-documented now. This chapter examined specific problems caused by specific insiders of the system as an illustration. More work of this nature is needed rather than the current academic, out-of-touch policies, interventions, and approaches that amount to mere intellectual masturbation. There is need for more urgent and practical actions and the will to challenge the powerful insiders, but not conveniently to keep playing along.

References

Belk, D. 2018. Conclusion: How did we get here and why is this so hard to fix? http://truecostofhealthcare.org/wp-content/uploads/2018/11/Conclusion.pdf

Dubois, B. 2010. Foreword. In W. Potter (ed.), *Deadly spin*, pp. ix–x. Bloomsbury Press: New York.

Folland, S., Goodman, A.C., & Stano, M. 2013. *The economics of health and health care.* Seventh Edition. Pearson: Upper Saddle River, NJ.

Gawande, A. 2009. The cost conundrum. *The New Yorker.* June 1.

Herzlinger, R. 2018. The IRS can save American health care. *The Wall Street Journal.* July 1.

Khatri, N., Pasupathy, K.S., & Hicks, L.L. 2012. The crucial role of people and information in health care organizations. In G.D. Brown, K.S. Pasupathy, & T. Patrick (eds.), *Health informatics: Transforming health care*, pp. 197–212. Health Administration Press: Chicago.

Komlos. J. 2017. Column: Here's what's wrong with the U.S. health care system. *PBS Newshour.* September 22.

Patashnik, E.M., Gerber, A.S., & Dowling, C.M. 2017. *Unhealthy politics: The battle over evidence-based medicine.* Princeton University Press: Princeton, NJ and Oxford.

Pearl, R. 2017. *Mistreated: Why we think we're getting good health care and why we're usually wrong.* Public Affairs: New York.

Potter, W. 2010. *Deadly spin.* Bloomsbury Press: New York.

Quadagno, J. 2008. Why the United States has no national health insurance: Stakeholder mobilization against the welfare state, 1945–1996. In C. Harrington & C.L. Estes (eds.), *Health policy: Crisis and reform in the U.S. health care delivery system*, pp. 419–426, Fifth Edition. Jones and Bartlett Publishers: Sudbury, MA.

Reinhardt, U.E. 2019. *Priced out: The economic and ethical costs of American health care*. Princeton University Press: Princeton, NJ.

Ronis, S.R. 2007. *Timelines into the future*. Hamilton Books: Lanham, MD.

Shaffer, K. 2017. Letter to the editor: Greed is the problem in our health care system. *Bristol Herald Courier*. March 23.

Shrank, W.H., Rogstad, T.L., & Parekh, N. 2019. Waste in the US health care system: Estimated costs and potential savings. *JAMA*, 322(15): 1501–1509.

13 Well-Informed Citizenry

Chapter 10 noted various falsehoods that the system insiders have successfully propagated over the years: the US has the best health care system in the world, everyone gets health care anyhow, there is no rationing or waiting for health care treatments in the US like other universal or single payer systems, the current US health care system is a free market system, the free market can resolve the problems in the US health care system, and the US health care system is basically healthy, so incremental change is the best to address its problems (Geyman, 2008). The truth is that the system is broken as elaborated amply in Chapters 1 to 10. Glen Melnick, a professor of health economics, befittingly describes the US health care system: "It's now so dysfunctional that I sometimes think the only solution is to blow the whole thing up. It's not like any market on Earth" (quoted in Rosenthal, 2017). The US health care system needs to be fixed urgently as it is causing a lot of problems to American society. Let us waste no more precious time in defending a system, which is out of control.

Starr (2011) offers a key insight into the US health care system dysfunction. The fight between special interests and the suffering masses would fit easily into a familiar populist picture of the world with one caveat. While the special interests – private health insurers, drug companies, hospitals, and physicians – profit from the health system, they alone are not responsible for maintaining it. The bias against any reform of the system also comes from a group of well-off American citizens, a protected public. No other major democracy created a financing system that provides the biggest tax breaks to the people with the best private insurance. The well-off Americans may not be satisfied with what they have, but they assume anything different will be worse. They nurse a deep distrust of change. The tax subsidies and benefits that they receive as part of their health care are invisible to them. The implicit attitude is that big government is good for me but not for you (Chapman, 2017).

DOI: 10.4324/9781003112204-16

It is not possible to have it all. The aversion of well-off Americans to this simple truism is not without consequences. Compared with other Western nations, America has more people without insurance; Americans spend far more of the national income on health care and are less happy with the system (Chapman, 2017). The affluent citizens with highly subsidized health insurance are one of the most formidable barriers to any reform in the US health care system. While it is not clear how to change the minds of this group of people, there is a big chunk of American public, those who have been at the receiving end of the dysfunctionality in the US health care system, who may be ready to do something to fix the health care system. They just need to be educated and informed about the problems in the US health care system and the purported solutions. A fraction of money that is spent on misinformation if spent on informing and educating citizens about the problems and solutions of the health care system dysfunction can make a big difference.

The other obstacle, often cited as a source of resistance to health care reform, is American culture/values, which is mere a red herring that the system insiders use and exploit. Reinhardt (2019) points out a couple of ironies as they pertain to American values and resulting resistance to health care reform. The first irony is that a single-payer health care insurance system is thought to be un-American, and hence unthinkable. Why then is the public Medicare system for America's elderly passed in 1965, a classic single-payer system run by the federal government with uniform fee schedules and rules applicable everywhere in the country, so popular? Upon closer analysis, Medicare emerges as the bright spot in an otherwise dysfunctional system. Because of its simplicity, Medicare's administrative costs are one-third of the private health insurance plans.

The second irony pertains to the idea that purely socialized medicine is un-American. This irony lies in Americans' loathing of the term 'socialized medicine'. There is a distinction between 'social insurance' and 'socialized medicine'. Some countries (e.g., Canada, Germany, Israel, Japan, the Netherlands, and Switzerland) operate social health insurance systems, but the health care delivery system is a mixture of public and private health care providers. In a purely socialized medicine, not only the health insurance system is under government control, but government also owns and operates health care production facilities. So, even if Medicare is extended to all Americans, it would still not be a purely socialized medicine since for-profit and not-for-profit health care providers would continue to deliver care. An example of an ideal health care system is the health services provided by Veteran Administration (VA) hospitals, which remain popular, and veterans are quite protective of the VA system, suggesting that Americans hate the words 'government' or 'socialism' or 'communist', but love the services and programs that are delivered well by the government. They hate these words perhaps because they have been bombarded with them often in the past through aggressive, fearmongering campaigns.

Americans are good people. They are yearning for a fair system like people elsewhere. This is not a big ask. They have been duped for too long by the system insiders and deserve a break.

The lifestyle and attitudes of Americans toward health care are said to be part of the US health care system's dysfunction. It is claimed that Americans eat too much junk food and do not exercise, seek care when they are too sick, are culturally narcissistic in that they deny the inevitability of death and end up consuming too much care in the last six months of their lives, and love new medical gadgets and technologies. While these arguments may be true to some extent, there is a lack of understanding of why such attitudes exist. The system's spin machine and the predominant biomedical model practiced in the US are far more potent explanations for Americans' attitudes and behaviors. Their attitudes and behaviors could be changed if there is a will to do so.

The single-minded focus in the biomedical model is on treating patients after they get sick. Prevention as an approach to good health care does not receive much attention. The biomedical model narrowly focuses on biological factors but does not account for psychological, environmental, and social influences. The model does not consider individual's lifestyle or their environment. There are clear consequences of doing so as America is a chronically ill nation and ranks high in poor lifestyle choices. Other developed nations spend twice as much on public health than they spend on medical care. In the US, it is exactly the opposite. Public health approaches emphasize preventive care and educating and informing people to stay fit and healthy. Thus, poor lifestyle choices of Americans could be attributed significantly to the system that emphasizes medical care when people have gotten sick rather than preventive care.

Before passing the buck of poor health in the US to ordinary citizens, the role of various system insiders in spawning conditions that lead to poor lifestyle choices and habits need to be examined. For example, it is long known that the biomedical model of care has serious deficiencies, but it remains prevalent because it is good for business. The more the people get sick, the more they would seek care.

The system insiders keep promoting narratives of miracle drugs, treatments, and technologies as they reflect well on the system being most modern and cutting edge. Local TV news almost daily includes a news segment extolling medical technologies and miracle drugs. Such narratives shape attitudes of public and make people feel that the system can keep them young and alive forever. They make citizens crave for and consume more medical technologies as a result. In short, the attitudes and lifestyles of public could be shaped with more information and education. The US spends $3.8 trillion annually on health care. A fraction of this money, if deployed in proper information and education campaigns, may make a big difference in achieving far better health outcomes for Americans.

Joe Biden rightly noted in his inaugural presidential speech that we must reject the culture in which facts themselves are manipulated and even manufactured. And given the power of social media and the spin machine, knowing how to decode spin has become as important as basic literacy and numeracy skills in today's media world that the citizens must master (Potter, 2010).

Conclusion

Americans do not deserve a health care system that they currently have. They are good people like people in other countries. They would like to have a simple and fair system. Unfortunately, they have been taken for a ride by the system insiders, who rather than informing and educating them, misguide, misinform, and fearmonger them: "Reform will happen when you as a patient, fully empowered with information, begin to assert your rights" (Leifer, 2014).

References

Chapman, S. 2017. Column: Why health care can't be fixed. *Chicago Tribune*. March 24.

Geyman, J.P. 2008. Myths as barriers to health care reform in the United States. In C. Harrington & C.L. Estes (eds.), *Health policy: Crisis and reform in the U.S. health care delivery system*, pp. 407–413, Fifth Edition. Jones and Bartlett Publishers: Sudbury, MA.

Leifer, J. 2014. *The myth of modern medicine: The alarming truth about American health Care*. Rowman & Littlefield: Lanham, MD.

Potter, W. 2010. *Deadly spin*. Bloomsbury Press: New York.

Reinhardt, U.E. 2019. *Priced out: The economic and ethical costs of American health care*. Princeton University Press: Princeton, NJ.

Rosenthal, E. 2017. *An American sickness: How healthcare became a big business and how you can take it back*. Penguin Press: New York.

Starr, P. 2011. *Remedy and reaction*. Yale University Press: New Haven.

Conclusion

The US health care system dysfunction has been a perennial problem for many decades and American society so far has not quite been able to resolve this puzzle. Although the per capita spending of $11,582 in the US is more than double that of other developed nations, health care outcomes in the US are no better than theirs. In other words, the US health care system consumes far more resources to produce the same outcomes as other countries. The rising rates of health care insurance premiums in the US eat into any rise in the real income of Americans, and health care insecurity remains a commonly unrecognized source of suffering for many Americans. Americans fear large medical bills more than they do a serious illness.

The technical (or health care organizing/structuring) solution to the health care problem is known and achievable. Americans have solved far knottier technical problems, for example, landing the man on the moon or landing a rover on the Mars. Proper organization and management of health care delivery in the US does not sound as intimidating as those challenges. The tricky, unresolvable aspect of the health care problem in the US remains political, but not technical. Other countries have had much greater success to contain health care costs without compromising on the safety or quality of patient care. Moreover, other countries offer access to all citizens unlike the US where a significant number of citizens do not have any health insurance.

The failure of the US in this regard could be attributed to a great extent to crony capitalism. The US health care system has been suffering a lot from it because of the immense influence of politicians and powerful system insiders (health insurers, hospitals, pharmaceuticals, physicians, and medical device makers). The slow accretion of protection arrangements organized by these powerful insiders has put brakes on the ability of the federal and state governments and the American society to reform the system. The US health care industry employs the

DOI: 10.4324/9781003112204-17

largest numbers of lobbyists and spends the most on lobbying among all the 13 US industrial sectors. The government regulatory agencies at both federal and state levels are 'captured' by the health industry interest groups meaning that the regulatory agencies respond to the interests of the industry not of the citizens.

Three studies have estimated the amount of waste/dysfunction in the US health care system. As per these studies, the waste in the system varies from 25 to 34 percent of the total annual health care spending in the US. Several other developed countries seem to have found a better solution to the health care problem than the US as they get same or better health care outcomes than the US by spending about half as much per capita and about half as much of their gross domestic product as the US. Thus, a waste in the US health care system as high as 50 percent of the overall health care expenditure does not seem implausible.

The latest study conducted in 2019 put a conservative estimate of the annual waste in the US health care system of about 25 percent of the total annual US health care spending of $3.8 trillion. According to this study, there are four main categories of waste. First, administrative complexity that accounts for $266 billion in annual waste. Administrative complexity arises mostly because of a wide variety and complexity of private health insurance plans. Thus, private health insurers are principally responsible for this waste. The second main category of waste in the system is pricing failures of health care procedures, drugs, and services. The annual waste in this category is estimated to be about $235 billion. This category of waste is driven mostly by drug companies, but hospitals and physicians too contribute to this category of waste. The third major category of waste, failures of care delivery and coordination, is estimated in the range of $130 billion to $244 billion annually. This category results chiefly from health care providers being poorly organized and coordinated and includes things like hospital-acquired conditions and adverse events, clinician-related inefficiencies, and unnecessary admissions and avoidable complications. The last major category of the waste consists of overtreatments costing the US taxpayers anywhere from $76 billion to $101 billion every year. Health care providers and physicians contribute mostly to this category of waste/dysfunction in the system.

Well thought-out guardrails are urgently needed to curb the brazenness of the powerful system insiders. Private health insurance plans come in a crazy variety, making their administration complex and expensive. Like other countries, the US must establish uniform insurance plans with standard fee schedules that are easy to administer. Private health insurers need a lot of adult supervision.

Drugs, treatments, and procedures are far more expensive in the US because drug companies, physicians, and hospitals have complete control over their prices. The federal government must establish a more just and fair institutional framework to oversee the prices of health care treatments and services.

Hospitals and physicians are responsible for unnecessary treatments and services. The fee-for-service model encourages overtreatments. The overall budgets for hospitals, fixed salaries for physicians, and monitoring of overtreatments by physicians are the mechanisms other countries are using effectively to control the overuse of medicine. The current system suffers from the problem of 'other people's money'. Free access to health care with no out-of-pocket requirements diminishes personal responsibilities, leaving no demand-side constraints. Price-conscious behavior, with the use of deductibles and co-pays, can be encouraged with little impact on health.

Organization and management of hospitals and other health care providers remain poor because hospital markets remain super concentrated, undermining any discipline that competition brings. Thus, the hospital markets have to be opened to more competition. At present, hospitals that provide poor but more expensive care get reimbursed more. Further, through lobbying legislators at both federal and state levels, hospitals and health care providers have avoided any scrutiny of pricing of their products and services. They extort patients via the charge master.

The US political system has become polarized and corrupt. The situation is made worse by the amount of money interest groups plow into the system to capture health policy. Crony capitalism needs to be the part of the discussion and overcoming its perverse effects a remedy to truly fixing the system. Businesses and interest groups have come to realize that the US political system is not functioning properly and they are partly to be blamed for it. Further, they understand that they need to step up and do something to reform it. The Supreme Court's Citizens United decision has unleashed dark money into the US politics and made the political system much worse. It must be repealed. Its destructive influence could be neutralized to some extent by the small donor revolution.

Obviously, health care markets in the US are functioning poorly. The present system is a refined form of a jungle raj rather than a properly regulated, functioning free market. It is not unlike many poorly governed systems that we see across the globe. The US health care system needs a proper institutional framework otherwise the system insiders would continue to plunder the American economy and citizens in the name of free market economy. The misguided belief in Americans that all markets are always and everywhere necessarily efficient is patently false. Clinging to an outdated ideology is harmful as evidenced by the unsatisfactory performance of the US health care system over many decades.

Americans do not deserve a health care system that they currently have. They are good people like people in other countries. They would like to have a simple and fair system. Unfortunately, they have been taken for a ride by the system insiders, who rather than informing and educating them, misguide, misinform, and fearmonger them. Reform will happen when well-informed citizens fully empowered with information begin to assert their rights.

Index

Administrative costs (complexity) 18, 21, 47, 51–53, 55, 103–104, 113, 117

American Medical Association (AMA) 34, 46–47, 61, 69, 76, 79, 106

Billing and coding 52, 58, 61, 63–65, 72, 104–106

Biomedical model 73, 79, 86–87, 90, 92, 114

Campaign contributions 21, 31, 32, 36, 38, 39, 43, 48, 51, 55, 57, 69, 72, 79, 82, 84, 95–97, 117–118

Capture of health policy 33, 40, 95–96, 100, 104, 116–118

Citizens' United 31, 96, 98

Company insurance model 47, 70, 79

Comparative effectiveness research 24, 25

Conflict of interest 74–75, 85

Cost conundrum 59, 107

Crony capitalism 12–16, 21, 25, 31, 38, 43, 57, 66, 69, 74, 95–100, 102, 116, 118

Emergency room (ER) services 58, 64–65

Evidence-based medicine 23, 33, 39, 58, 78

Facility fee 64

Fads 20

Failures of care delivery 18, 57, 65, 71, 103, 107–108, 117

Fee-for service 70, 79, 107–108, 118

Food and Drug Administration (FDA) 25, 38, 40, 43, 84, 105–106

Front groups 49–50, 69, 72

Gawande 26–27, 59, 71, 79, 109

Generic drugs 43

Grassroots groups 49–50, 69, 72

Grifting 31

Guidelines by medical specialties 27

Health care costs (comparison across countries) 4

Health care insecurity 4

Health care reform 46–48, 50–51, 69–70, 78, 89, 95–100, 119

Health care premiums 4, 9

Health care spending in US 3

Hippocratic oath 73

Hospital acquired infections 19, 65, 107

Hospital charge master 60, 65, 106, 118

Hospitals 21, 26, 32, 45, 48, 52–52, 57–58, 63, 69, 77, 88, 92, 96, 102, 104–108, 112, 116, 118

Intellectual masturbation 20

Interest groups 31, 32, 35

Institutional corruption 74

Institutional sclerosis 35

Insurance companies 21, 26, 32, 34, 45, 47–48, 52, 54, 58, 62, 64,

69–70, 78, 88–90, 96, 102, 104, 112, 116–117

Lobbying 21, 32, 36, 48, 95–97, 117
Lobbying by hospitals 57
Lobbying by insurance companies 51, 55
Lobbying my medical device makers 82, 84
Lobbying by pharmaceuticals 38, 39, 43, 105–106
Lobbying by physicians 69, 72, 79

Market concentration (power) 33, 52–53, 55, 57, 62, 65, 83, 105–107, 118
Mayo Clinic 59–60, 65, 71, 107
Medical devices 25–26, 34, 54, 75, 78, 82–84
Medical homes 19
Malpractice tort 77
Medicare/Medicaid 46–47, 52, 55, 58–59, 61, 63, 76, 104, 107, 113
Misinformation 46, 49–50, 61, 65, 84, 86, 87–89, 92, 104, 110, 113–114, 119

Opioid crisis 8, 42
Overtreatments 19, 26–27, 58–59, 65, 71, 74–75, 77, 87, 91, 103, 108, 117–118

Patashnik et al. 23–25, 33, 58, 71, 78–79, 86–87, 91–92, 103
Pharmaceutical benefit manager (PBM) 25, 41
Pharmaceutical companies 25–27, 32, 34–35, 38–39, 45, 47, 54, 58, 69,

75, 78, 82, 88, 92, 96, 102, 105–106, 112, 116, 118
Physical therapy 65
Physicians 26, 32, 34, 39–40, 45, 54, 58, 60, 62, 88, 91, 96, 102, 104–106, 108, 112, 116, 118
Politicians/interest groups 31, 32, 35
Potter 45, 47–48, 50–51, 53, 55, 70, 90, 109, 115
Precision medicine 19
Price transparency 60, 63–65, 84, 105–107
Pricing failures 18, 103, 105, 117

Regulatory capture 33, 40, 95–96, 100, 104, 116–118
Reinhardt 45, 52–53, 60, 88, 104, 113
Relative Value Scale Update Committee 76
Relative Value Units (RVUs) 59
Rosenthal 23, 34, 38, 43, 60–61, 65, 71, 77–78, 82

Scam 9
Single-payer system 51–52, 70, 72, 91, 112–113
Socialism or socialized medicine 20–21, 46, 86, 88, 90, 102–103, 112–114
Specialty medical societies 34
Spin machine 50, 87–90, 104, 114–115, 119

Translational science 19

Value-based purchasing 19

Waste in US health care system 6, 9, 17–21, 55, 58, 78, 103, 110

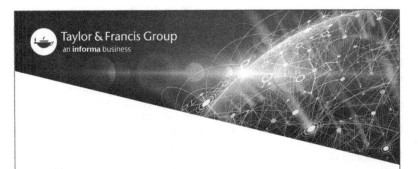